Epitaph to Indirect Rule

First published in 1956, *Epitaph to Indirect Rule* compares the old order of colonial government, represented by the Indirect Rule system, with the innovations of the more democratic administrative pattern introduced in the Eastern Region of Nigeria for the first time in 1950. Mr Akpan gives an account of the composition, powers, responsibilities, and financing and staffing of local government; and discusses the problems of supervision and control of the village, District, and other Councils under the new system. The author not only draws upon English experiences, but also gives a brief description of practices of local government adopted by other countries of the world—Ireland, France, Sweden, and the USA. This book will be of interest to students and researchers of African studies.

I0025544

Epitaph to Indirect Rule

A Discourse on Local Government in Africa

Ntieyong U. Akpan

Routledge
Taylor & Francis Group

First published in 1956
by Frank Cass and Company Limited

This edition first published in 2024 by Routledge
4 Park Square, Milton Park, Abingdon, Oxon, OX14 4RN

and by Routledge
605 Third Avenue, New York, NY 10017

Routledge is an imprint of the Taylor & Francis Group, an informa business

© 1956 Ntieyong U. Akpan

Publisher's Note
The publisher has gone to great lengths to ensure the quality of this reprint but points out that some imperfections in the original copies may be apparent.

Disclaimer
The publisher has made every effort to trace copyright holders and welcomes correspondence from those they have been unable to contact.

A Library of Congress record exists under LCCN: 67103746

ISBN: 978-1-032-85458-8 (hbk)
ISBN: 978-1-003-51827-3 (ebk)
ISBN: 978-1-032-85461-8 (pbk)

Book DOI 10.4324/9781003518273

EPITAPH TO INDIRECT RULE

A Discourse on Local Government in Africa

NTIEYONG U. AKPAN

FRANK CASS & CO. LTD.
1967

Published by
FRANK CASS AND COMPANY LIMITED
67 Great Russell Street, London WC1
by arrangement with Cassell and Company Limited

First edition	1956
New impression	1967

Printed in Great Britain by
Thomas Nelson (Printers) Ltd., London and Edinburgh

Dedicated

with sadness and affection, to

my beloved late wife, Grace Akpan (*née* Essien), who died suddenly
in London during the writing of this book

and to

the Rev. A. T. H. Taylor, M.A., B.D., a Scottish Missionary in
Calabar, in gratitude for his Christian help and financial sacrifice
in giving the author, who was an orphan, his primary and
secondary education, as well as providing him with other needs
and protection during that time.

CONTENTS

INTRODUCTION

READERS are entitled to a brief explanation as to why and how this book came to be written. I am an administrative officer serving the Eastern Regional Government of Nigeria. (I am also, it might interest readers to know, a native of that part of Africa.) My duties are such that I am in a position to observe at close quarters how the new local government bodies have been working. At one time I had the privilege of serving in an area where there had not as yet been a changeover from the 'Indirect Rule' to the more democratic system of local government.

The Eastern Region of Nigeria, it should be remembered, was the first colonial territory in Africa where a wholesale experiment in democratic form of local government, based on the English pattern and practice, was boldly started—a radical departure from the accustomed system of Native Administration or Indirect Rule. The change was in character both sweeping and complete. The first Local Government Ordinance giving effect to this development was passed in 1950. Reforms have also taken place in the Gold Coast and the Western Region of Nigeria where new Local Government Ordinances, more or less following the pattern of the one for the Eastern Region of Nigeria, have been passed.

The reforms were generally welcomed by the people. The new councillors entered upon their new responsibilities with ardent enthusiasm. But, alas, this enthusiasm was soon to be dampened; for the councillors shortly discovered that not only were their duties far from being as easy as they might have anticipated, but also that their popularity among their people was seriously dwindling. Their difficulties were very much increased by the hostile attitude of those they were serving. Within a short period, a great deal happened which could easily prove fatal to the whole system of Local Government. This would be a serious political as well as social calamity for the nation, since it would mean the destruction of the two chief aims of Local Government touched upon in the first chapter of this book.

The difficulties thus confronting our new local government bodies were a matter of grave concern to many people. If the difficulties merely constituted passing phases—that is to say, did not go to the root of the whole set-up—there was not too much to be worried about: riots could be put down if they occurred through ignorance on the part of the people as a result of the well-intentioned decisions and actions of the local councillors; and those failing, for instance, to pay the lawful rates demanded by the authorities might be adequately punished. But if, as many people (including the writer) soon became convinced, something was basically wrong and needed correction or readjustment in the whole set-up, the effects of such measures could only be very temporary—and might even be destroyed altogether through frequent resort to punitive measures. I began to think; my thoughts led to study and investigation; and I finally conceived the idea of this book.

Now the development of democratic or representative forms of local government in Africa has, since the end of the last war, been a matter of considerable thought, not only in the colonies but also in Britain. There has been a certain amount of literature on the subject—there is for instance Mr. Wraith's book, *Local Government* (published by Penguin) which deals with West Africa, not to mention the various articles which have appeared in the Press.

The aim has generally been to ask, from the background of English experience, searching and guiding questions capable of helping the peoples to find answers to their own problems. There has as yet been no attempt to tackle the questions generally from an African background, which shows that a book attempting to do this, no matter how imperfectly, cannot be out of place or superfluous.

It is, however, needless to stress the important point that many of the answers attempted in this book are necessarily tentative, although it is honestly believed that they can at least lead to the finding of real answers in many areas. It is also important to bear in mind that the aim is far from being an attempt to tackle all the questions which have been asked on the subject—that would require a volume many times the size of the present one, even if it were possible to do so. Again, attempted answers to questions constitute only *an aim* of the book, for it also contains a few questions of its own as well as some criticisms.

It follows that, highly tentative though many points raised in this book may be, they can easily become controversial, since it has meant advocating a substantial departure from custom in many cases. I see no harm in raising such a controversy, should it be inevitable, provided it can stimulate serious thought, study and research into the different problems involved. But this does not mean that my sole purpose has been to raise controversy—of which I would naturally be afraid. The arguments have not been thrown out as a mere matter of brain exercise, but are the legitimate children of my own convictions reached after considerable and disinterested thought and study. If I have any appeal to make it is that readers should keep an open mind in reading and appraising the various arguments, as I have done in putting them forward.

As should be easily understood, I have found it necessary for the purpose of illustrations, to make use of known facts. This has meant making frequent references to experiences in England, and to a still greater extent of experiences in Eastern Region of Nigeria. In this latter case, I have used the provisions of the old Ordinance (about to be amended or repealed) and experiences under it—and it is better to use this 'dead' ordinance so as to remove any imputations that this book is limited to one part of Africa. For I believe that the experiences and thoughts contained in this book will be useful to other African colonies which may consider the reforms of their own systems.

Just a word about two items included in this book: first,

Chapter X contains a brief description of what exists in other countries of the world—to wit, Ireland, France, Sweden and the U.S.A. This is done in order to draw attention to these systems—or rather practices under them —which may provide useful lessons for some territories. It has been adequately shown in the book how unwise it would be to depend entirely on the English experience which is itself undergoing active and most desirable reform. The second point is that, in Appendix A, I have discussed the future position of Administrative Officers as servants of the Central Government. This has been a most risky and delicate thing to do, but it was felt that, since their relationship with local government bodies has been given a good space in the main body of the book, their position as Central Government officials might also be discussed, as it is important that their position in one capacity should not be lost sight of when discussing their position in the other capacity.

Finally, it is of the utmost importance to make it absolutely clear that, although I am a serving official, nothing in this book should be taken as necessarily reflecting, either directly or indirectly, official opinions.

For their encouragement I am deeply grateful to many friends and well-wishers, especially to Mr. R. E. Wraith and Dr. L. P. Mair of the London School of Economics. My thanks are also due to the Eastern Regional Government for making it possible for me to visit London for six months, thus enabling me to gain access to invaluable library facilities as well as to establish useful contacts. I should also like to place on record my appreciation of the willingness of my European friends to answer any question I put to them about their own systems.

Finally, my greatest indebtedness is due to my late but ever to be remembered and respected wife, Grace, without whose company, encouragement, and assistance it would not have been possible to complete this book within the very short time in which it was done.

N. U. A.

London, January 1955

CHAPTER I

BACKGROUND AND BASIS

THE end of the Second World War brought in its train many changes, many problems, many duties and new responsibilities. The changes were far-reaching and revolutionary, while the problems, duties and responsibilities were great and perplexing. These affected practically all countries of the world, whether they had directly taken part in the war or not; but to Great Britain the effects came with particularly pressing force and interest, for she had not only herself to consider but her dependent oversea territories as well. The spontaneous and loyal efforts of these oversea territories in helping to bring the war to a successful conclusion had produced a profound and cumulative effect on the British attitude towards them. The importance and needs of the colonies now appeared in a strikingly new light. 'A will to return the spontaneous help that flowed in from the colonies [during the war] worked a favourable change in the British attitude, assuring active support for proposals to help them.' (Macmillan: *Africa Emergent*, p. 267.) More, perhaps, than the need merely to return thanks to the colonies, Britain saw in the colonies a new source of strength and resources which should with mutual advantage be developed and sustained. Political, economic and social development of these colonies accordingly became an urgent concern of the British Government.

This, of course, is not to say that the aim was completely lacking until after the war. Indeed the original British attitude that the chief mission in Africa was to give law, order and protection as well as natural justice to the natives had begun, during the twenties, to develop into one of active *partnership* with the territories concerned. This, in effect, meant an acknowledgement by Britain that it was part of her responsibility in Africa to develop and make the territories grow economically and socially. This new attitude was first given expression in the Colonial Development Act of 1929, reinforced by that of 1940. The experiences of the Second World War gave more life and impetus to this belief; and the Colonial Development and Welfare Act of 1945 was but a translation of this strengthened belief into positive action.

In the political field the old-fashioned idea that the African was not worthy of the vote, in other words, was not capable of enjoying democratic form of government, became at once out of date and untenable. As in economic and social fields, political development in the colonies was given new life and impetus after the war. The proper place to sow the seeds for the inevitable political development was seen to lie at the local government level, as was clearly stated in the following passage in a report entitled *The Colonial Empire* (1939–47) presented to Parliament by the Secretary of State in July 1947:

> The encouragement of local political interest and the building up of a system of efficient and democratic (later changed for 'representative') local government is a cardinal feature of British policy in Africa. It is now recognized that the political progress of the territories is dependent on the development of responsibility in local government, that without sound local government a democratic political system at the centre is not possible, and that, if social services are to be built up and expanded, there must be efficient organs of local government directly representative of the people to operate and control them.

It is with this aspect of post-war development in the colonies, namely, *local government*, that this book is going to deal.

The above passage shows two distinctive aims for local government development, namely:

(*a*) *Political*—It must provide training ground for eventual democratic self-government at the centre.

14

(*b*) *Social*—It must provide a basis for the provision and operation or expansion of social services.

For these two aims to be achieved, whatever system is evolved should be 'efficient and representative'. Neither of the above two aims was a course entirely new to local government in Africa, and it is important that one should never lose sight of this fact. The passage does not suggest, it is possible to say, that what was envisaged was the *introduction* of entirely new systems. It has happened that in some areas where this policy of the Secretary of State for the Colonies is pursued with the highest priority and vigour, attention has had first of all to be cast elsewhere for lessons —to Europe or even other parts of Africa; which is not at all a bad idea provided it is done in such a way that the impression is not given that an entirely new thing, unknown to the people before, is going to be *imported* or *introduced*. The unique advantage that Africa has over Europe or even America, pioneers in the same fields, is that it is able to learn and profit by both the mistakes and successes of these older countries.

In a certain part of Africa the implementation of this policy was seized upon by the authorities, *and the people*, as a golden opportunity—and so it was—for providing a long-felt and urgent need for reform in an area where, lacking in strong centralized indigenous authorities, the orthodox Native Administration system could not work satisfactorily. To do this, various preliminary steps were taken—consultation of the people and examination of other systems. After much work and thought, it was decided that the area in question could 'usefully profit by the English experience without necessarily attempting to imitate the English system in detail'. The area concerned could indeed 'usefully *profit by the English experience*', but there are people who are somewhat doubtful as to whether the reforms which followed did not actually *borrow too much of the British practice* at the expense of some important local essentials.

The adoption of the English system in that apparently fertile area has, however, succeeded as reasonably as could be expected, but, nevertheless, one would have liked to see it made a little more *local*, by taking into account facts of historical process, of local circumstances, and of local administrative needs—things which were completely unknown to English people and therefore could not affect their system which, incidentally, is itself under active consideration for reform!

In studying any system of local government in the world, sight should not be lost of the important fact that such a system is peculiar to that particular country, and as such it might be useful, during such study, to watch for the mistakes and defects in that system to ensure that such mistakes are not repeated in whatever reforms are contemplated in any other country, though at the same time not closing the eyes against any good features which might be usefully borrowed for *adaptation*. And adaptation would imply taking into account (to put it metaphorically) the different 'climatic' (politically speaking) conditions in different areas. That would be about the best way of really profiting from other peoples' experience.

Here one is bound to be reminded of the easy danger of copying. The risk of doing it is very common at a time when different people are tackling the same problems simultaneously, for, once some solution is found in one place, there is always the strong tendency for others to rush and borrow a leaf. The Indirect Rule *practice* (as opposed to *principle* which, by itself, would have enabled the practice to be modified in each case according to local circumstances) was lustily copied everywhere in Africa with, of course, varying degrees of success and failure. We should not necessarily want to go the same way again with the new reforms. Let us accept a common principle but have, if necessary, different practices.

Writing of the old and now-dying parent system, Dr. L. P. Mair in *Native Policies in Africa* (p. 15) states that 'the real meaning of Indirect Rule cannot be summed up in the phrase "Find the chief". *It consists in an understanding of the structure of the native society and the interrelation of its parts, which precludes the possibility of assuming that it can be suddenly modernized from the outside, and at the same time reveals the points at which changed circumstances call for readjustment, and the bases on which necessary innovations can be firmly established.'* (Italics ours.) For, as another writer points out, 'any given civilization, however primitive, in Africa as in Europe, has a life of its own. It consists of people who have grown up with certain ideas, certain ties, obligations, expectations, and a certain relation with their own government. Any sudden and violent change in such a civilization, or its method of government, is like the dislocation of a human body. It breaks what was a living and homogeneous social unit, possibly crude and simple in form, but self-respecting and energetic, into a mere scattering of human units, despondent and usually corrupt.' (Cary: *Britain and West Africa*, p. 54.)

There can hardly be better working principles to follow in the new reforms, than those which these eminent writers, who know what they are talking about, have put forward. It is perhaps regrettable that, very often in the haste to carry out the reforms in answer to orders from above, those on the spot are obliged to pay too little attention to such principles. The answer to modern needs cannot lie in the question, 'What is happening there?' but rather in, 'What is happening here? How far have we got? What are our peculiar circumstances? And where can we go from here?' The search for proper answers to these questions will almost certainly lead to proper solutions based on local needs, and thus would make what may result truly 'local governments', and not just copied or superimposed systems. That would prevent such mistakes, for instance, as assuming that since there are no central government officials (like the D.O. or D.C. in Africa) in Britain the new local government systems now evolving should necessarily preclude them.

That would preclude any 'attempt . . . to make as it were, a crown or a king at the top and then try to find something underneath on which it might—perhaps—appropriately be placed'. (Sir Donald Cameron: *Native Administration in Nigeria and Tanganyika*.)

The development of local government in Africa should be looked upon as a continuous and growing process and not just as a once-and-for-all achievement. Societies are never static, unless they are dead, and so social institutions cannot be final and static. Whatever reforms, therefore, take place should be regarded as but a phase in that evolutionary process which has been at work ever since the introduction of Native Administration, or Indirect Rule, system into Africa. The fact that in the places where the reforms are taking place the term 'Local Government' has been substituted for the former one·of 'Native Administration' is merely a reflection of popular wish and does not in any way indicate that 'Local Government' did not exist before. The word 'Native' had become unpopular amongst Africans who saw in it a suggestion of inferior status, and so something more acceptable had to be substituted for it. There could have been no central government without a system of local government—which might take any form, from the system of central government officials administering the areas in person, to one where these officials act behind the scenes; from a system of sole native authorities in the persons of chiefs or a council of chiefs, to a system of democratically elected and constituted councils, and so on. Where the reforms or developments are not based on this understanding they are most likely to be seriously undermined from the start, since they would then appear to have no foundation or basis, but to be just something dropping, as it were, from the skies. If anything needs solid foundation—which may mean a certain degree of tradition—upon which to build, it is political development; and the people for whom these reforms are being undertaken should from the start be made to appreciate this important fact. Failure to acknowledge and make this fact known early enough in the process of development may lead to undesirable results. One such result would be, as indeed has actually happened somewhere, for the electors to deprive the new councils of men of ability and experience, men who might have happened to have played some part in the old system of Native Administration. The loss, in this way, of good talent and useful experience to the new bodies would be unfortunate for the much desired efficiency.

It would be useful at this stage to remind ourselves of some of the influences that led to the developments and reforms now under consideration.

It has already been seen how the war brought about a radical change in the British attitude towards her colonies. The same war had taken the colonials to different parts of the world where they acquired new experience and, perhaps more important to them, shared everything in common with their British comrades, not as masters and servants, but as friends and equals. They went back to their respective countries with memories of this new experience of friendship and equality, and naturally joined in the demand for the extension of such relationship into civil fields, thus giving invaluable support to great national leaders. The most effective way by which this could be done was for the ruling or tutelary power to grant political advancement to the territories concerned. The same war had as its motto 'World's Freedom' for which the colonial soldiers and people believed they were fighting. Like the French soldiers who had helped the American colonies in their fight against Britain for Independence, they developed a new taste and meaning for freedom which they would like to see in their own countries. They saw it as a sort of injustice that an external power, no matter how benevolent, should deny them greater freedom in the management of their own internal affairs. The same war had produced the 'Atlantic Charter' the text of which, though differently interpreted on both sides of the Atlantic by the principal signatories, provided a strong source of faith and hope for the colonial people.

Tied to all these considerations was Britain, whose attitude *vis-à-vis* the colonies had already begun to take a new turn.

In the colonies themselves, the British officials, desirous of accelerating the pace of their professed policy—the education of the people towards representative, democratic and efficient self-government—strongly felt that the time had come for some reforms in the method of local administration, particularly in those areas where, lacking strong centralized authorities, the ground was fairly fertile and ready for the seeds to be planted. In this they derived encouragement and inspiration from general conditions in the colonies where old societies were disintegrating, giving place to new ones; where the positions of traditional authorities were being challenged by the rising educated middle classes, and where constitutional reforms were taking shape. Let us give passing glances at these last influences in the colonies.

Increased trade, improved communications and growing desire for wealth and experience had resulted in the influx of 'expatriate natives' into other tribal territories. The direct result of this was the expansion of cosmopolitan towns, peopled by different communities. In some of these towns the 'stranger' populations were considerable compared with those of the indigenous natives, and normally comprised traders, people in various forms of employment, professionals, and even retired people who decided to settle in the locality permanently. These people contributed, very substantially, perhaps even more than the indigenous inhabitants in some cases, to the general development of the locality—by way of taxes and rates, by putting up modern buildings, by setting up farming, trading or industrial establishments, etc. It would be definitely unfair—indeed impossible—to exclude these people permanently from having a say in the day to day conduct of affairs in the communities where they had so much at stake, and were bound to be affected by the actions and decisions of the authority in control of the area. The only way of giving them the desired say in local affairs was to give them representation on local councils, and this meant relaxation in the principles and tenets of *local government by indigenous traditional authorities.*

With the rise of the educated middle classes in the various territories, the old forms of native authorities have tended to lose both in popularity and effectiveness. This is well known; for in all the colonies agitation for reform has come most strongly, and one would add effectively, from the educated middle classes through the press and other means of expression. They have come, with real justification in most cases, to look upon the old local authority set-ups as unprogressive and inefficient. Where necessary, they have even gone to the extent of leading organized opposition against the chiefs. Their education has not only armed them with means of livelihood and independence from the chiefs, but has liberalized their minds from excessive traditional reverence towards their chiefs, whom they can now openly criticize and want to replace. They are more and more availing themselves of new opportunities at the expense of old obligations.

This trend is understandable; for the original functions and position of the chief tend to have little or no place at all in modern societies. Two of such original functions are particularly affected—his functions as a war leader and as a family or tribal priest. The first is completely out of the question nowadays, while the second is only recognized by sections, very often insignificant sections, of the community in the face of present Christian civilization and influences. His other two important functions are not yet completely lost, although very considerably weakened; and these are settling of disputes and serving as a symbol of unity and tradition. This last function or position, if constitutionally regulated, is still generally accepted by the majority of people, and is likely to be the only function that will remain for many years to come if the chiefs themselves are prepared, willing and capable of adapting themselves wisely to new conditions. The tendency now, in some parts of Nigeria for instance, appears to be to make the positions of the chiefs purely constitutional, and there have been cases where those who feel they cannot adapt themselves successfully to the new conditions are beginning to abdicate *sua sponte*. *All this does not, of course, mean that the influence of these chiefs in local affairs has disappeared—indeed, as we shall see in a later chapter, such an erroneous conception can easily bring difficulties, if not disaster, to the cause of local government reforms.* The important need is to proceed with the greatest caution and tact in the process of adapting the position of the chiefs to modern conditions.

Lastly we come to the introduction of such constitutional reforms as what was known as the *Richards Constitution* in Nigeria. In a paper read by Sir Bernard Bourdillon, former Governor and Commander-in-Chief of Nigeria, before ever the *Richards Constitution* was formulated or published, the following passage appears:

> I should like to call attention to the necessity for a closer connection between the Native Authorities and the central legislature. . . . The time has not yet come, and will not come as yet, when the Nigerian peasant will be capable of electing his own representatives to the legislature, and the present unofficial members, whether elected or nominated, do not really sufficiently represent the peasant class. The professional, salaried and trading classes are amply represented, but not the primary producer. The Native Authorities are, however, fully alive to his interests, and can be trusted to look after them if they are fully represented in the legislature.

Whether Native Authorities, as they were then constituted, could be said to be fully representative of the peasant farmer or primary producer is open to further consideration, but the main point of interest in the passage lies in the fact that the *Richards Constitution*, introduced not long afterwards, did in fact bring the Native Authorities into closer connection with the central legislature, for under it

Native Authorities formed themselves into electoral colleges for the election of representatives to the central legislature. As a result of this new requirement something rather interesting presented itself. The majority of the chiefs constituting the Native Authorities were illiterate, and would be definitely valueless in the central legislature where education and command of the English language were necessary. The Native Authorities themselves fully appreciated this fact and, very remarkably, *themselves* found a way out by bringing about the creation of new chiefs from the educated ranks of their societies. These new chiefs were then admitted into the native administration councils and eventually elected to represent the respective Native Authorities in the central legislature. Once the door was in this way opened into the Native Administration councils for younger educated elements it could never be closed again.

The above may be described as the most immediate forces. They did not by themselves give birth to the idea that change was necessary, but merely revived in a very strong and irresistible way a feeling that had been ever present in the minds of various people, official and unofficial alike, for many years past.

The real problem to be faced in respect of the present and future new systems will not lie merely in the setting up of councils, which may be democratic or representative enough, but on how to make these councils also efficient. In the past there was frequently the tendency to allow the aim of making local government a basis for general political training to override all else, so that inefficiency and waste through inexperience and inability on the part of the councillors were regarded as a necessary corollary of such training and therefore tolerated. It was often argued in excuse that a child could not walk without trying to do so without the protection of the mother; and trying in this way meant occasionally falling and bruising itself which in turn would make it learn to be more careful next time. In the same way the new local councils could not get to know their work without trying and making mistakes. This is quite true, but there is the risk of venturing too far.

The second main aim of local government development is that it should be a basis for the provision or expansion of social services. Foundations for these have already been laid in the old system. The needs are growing much faster than the meagre resources at the disposal of the new local government bodies. This calls for a good deal of efficient administration of the business and funds of these councils, and shows the need to check anything which may lead to excessive inefficiency and waste. To do this will certainly require some control and guidance from the more experienced staff of the central government. This control and guidance may only be temporary, but it is bound to be necessary for some time. The degree and method of control (we might call it supervision) and guidance will be governed by local needs. Experience under the long tried N.A. system has shown that 'where Native Authorities were left with a degree of independence which made effective supervision by the central government difficult or impossible, their greater "freedom" often meant freedom to misgovern, failure to adapt themselves to fast-changing social and economic conditions'. (Batten: *Problems of African Development*, Part II, p. 118.) It is doubtful if this situation can be suddenly altered for the better by the mere fact that the new councils are going to be mostly elective, with men of education and talent, but not necessarily with much or any experience, serving on them.

CHAPTER II

EPITAPH TO INDIRECT RULE

INDIRECT Rule system has in late years been the subject of much study, much criticism (adverse and favourable) and much literature. These have come from what may be described as *interested* and *disinterested* parties. As a result, new theories and explanations of it have been evolved or expounded, particularly by those who have been studying the system constructively. Some of these new theories or expositions would, indeed, deeply impress if not surprise its originators who, it is possible to say, might have had fairly different conceptions. Amongst the interested students may be included those in whose countries the system has been practised, as well as those whose duty it is or has been officially to administer the system. Amongst the *disinterested* students are those who have impartially studied the system from the outside, and being themselves outside the thick woods can perhaps see what those who are actually inside may not be able to see. This latter class of students should at least be expected to form their judgements without much prejudice—subject to some allowances, of course.

These 'disinterested' students of the system, and, for that matter, some of the interested ones too, have in the recent past, given it really positive and progressive conceptions and interpretations. Unfortunately, though understandably, these new theories have in the past hardly impressed the rising generations of educated nationals of the African territories concerned. The new theories and the new generation of educated nationals almost simultaneously came into prominence in the early 'thirties of this century and have both since been growing together, and that may be a partial explanation of why it is difficult for one to appreciate the other.

The educated nationalists saw in the system nothing but an imperialistic device on the part of the governing power by which the subject races might be kept down for ever, or at least indefinitely. (There were some, of course, of the more discerning among these nationalists who were prepared to admit that there was some good in the system, although they strongly disapproved of its machinery.) The unfortunate thing about it all was the very strong tendency on the part of very powerful sections of the educated communities not to appreciate the real merits of the system. As has been said this tendency could at the same time be easily understood for a number of reasons, the most fundamental of which may be said to include the following:

(i) The original motives behind the European scramble for Africa, clearly borne out by the Berlin Conference of 1885, were well-known and could not be said to be honourable to African races. The parties to the Berlin Partition of Africa hardly had—or pretended to have—as their principal aim the development of the African continent *for the benefit of the African races*. Rather, their professed motive appeared to be the acquisition of African territories as a means of national prestige, wealth and power for the acquiring nations. Against Britain this fact appeared particularly underlined by her immediate step of handing over the administration of these territories, in the first place, to commercial companies, chartered, or formed and chartered, soon after the Berlin Conference for the purpose. Unlike, for instance, the Charter granted to the East India Company in 1600 the new charters did not require the Companies concerned to leave the natives and their territories alone and concentrate on trade, but rather the companies were required to make the administration and control of these territories one—perhaps an overriding one—of their principal concerns. Captain Lugard, later Lord Lugard, the first Governor-General of Nigeria and the generally accepted author of the Indirect Rule System, was originally

26

a soldier in the private employ of the Royal Niger Company. The fact that Britain, where opinion on the desirability of colonial expansion was divided (sharply divided until about 1860) at the time, was clearly encouraged by humanitarian and religious influences did not quite materially affect the position from the point of view of Africans, some of whom, while gratefully appreciating the really good and lasting work of these humanitarian and religious bodies in Africa, tended to be somewhat sceptical as to whether these bodies might not after all have been a sort of camouflaging complement to the imperial plan.

(ii) It could be argued in some quarters that the system of Indirect Rule was not, in its origin, specifically designed for the benefit, or even in the interest, of the natives but was rather a child of necessity. The writings of Lord Lugard himself, and of his most outstanding disciple, Sir Donald Cameron, tend, unconsciously no doubt, to lend colour to this belief. For both agree that limited resources, in manpower and finance, made any attempt at direct rule, in Nigeria for instance, quite impracticable and so a system whereby the territory could be administered and controlled with any passable effectiveness had to be adopted. A writer—incidentally an 'interested' party in favour of the system—has suggested that Lugard in fact borrowed a leaf from, or merely developed, the practice already tried in the southern part of Nigeria where Sir George Goldie, as chairman of the Niger Company, had in 1879 (i.e. many years before the Company was chartered or Lugard came into prominence) instructed his officials that 'if *the welfare of the native races is to be* considered, if dangerous revolts are to be obviated, the general principle of ruling on African principles, through native rulers, must be followed *for the present*'.[1] (The sections italicized leave one in doubt about supporting the argument one way or the other without proper study of the documents themselves. 'Welfare' is a very vague word and what exactly did Goldie mean by it?

[1] Cary, *Britain and West Africa* (p. 53).

27

His own conception of 'welfare for the native races' might easily have meant quite a different thing from what modern Africa could accept. England herself in 1879 had, in fact, conceptions of welfare for her own people quite different from present-day conceptions. Again, what did the words 'for the present' really signify? Resort to direct rule as soon as conditions became favourable? This might appear to be supported by the expressed need to 'obviate dangerous revolts'. 'Indirect Rule', however, for all its faults, and in spite of whatever might have been the original motive behind it, was much more to be preferred, as better for the natives, than any form of 'Direct Rule' would have been. Another useful—though purely academic—point brought out by the above quotation, is the apparent suggestion that the birthplace of Indirect Rule was after all the south and not the north of Nigeria, and that Goldie and not Lugard was its real author.)

(iii) Another argument has been that, even granting that the preceding argument is rejected, the system in practice could not possibly be for the progress of the territories concerned, since it merely favoured, sheltered and strengthened illiterate, conservative, unprogressive and sometimes autocratic chiefs at the expense of younger educated elements who, admitted into the Native Administration Councils, would be better able to understand and follow what was going on in the Councils as well as be able to take bold initiative in matters with which the councils might be concerned.

(iv) One other point of disgust about the system was the apparent policy to keep the Administrative Service, to which the system was intricately tied, exclusively for expatriates under the belief, rightly or wrongly, that no indigenous African was suitable for admission into it. An eloquent expression of national feelings in this respect was given by Dr. Namdi Azikiwe in his *Political Blueprint of Nigeria* published in 1943, in which the following statements appear (pp. 16–17):

It is true that I have already discussed the Civil Service of Nigeria, but I wish to make it clear that, at present, the Administrative Service is almost a separate department from the rest of Government departments in Nigeria. From time immemorial it was regarded as a sacrosanct institution from whose ranks indigenous Nigerians were barred. It is true that there have been isolated instances when Nigeria nationals were appointed Administrative Officers, but if one should say that these people were tolerated, that is not stretching the point. . . . Nigerians have often viewed with alarm the tendency of the Colonial Office to impose on them alien political officers in the Administrative Service, with the result that in certain instances alien ideologies have replaced indigenous political philosophy of government and administration, despite the worship of the political cult of the so-called 'Indirect Rule'.

Later, on page 21 of the same booklet, Dr. 'Zik' states:

Admittedly, there is some good in the 'Indirect Rule' system but, in practice, some of the problems raised, and the attempted solutions to them—legal, political and social, etc.— have given ground for justified apprehensions.

(v) Mention of 'political cult' brings to mind one strong psychological factor. The Indirect Rule system was based on the somewhat doubtful principle of 'letting the natives alone to develop in their own ways'. Such a policy *prima facie* clearly discouraged any definite attempt to *develop* the natives into advanced cultural, political, economic and social standards anywhere near what the Europeans were enjoying. It led in real practice to a sort of quasi-apartheid policy in the colonial territories, where Europeans hardly associated with the natives; lived apart from the natives, had separate clubs, separate hospitals, in some place even separate churches, to which no African, no matter what his social standing, could be admitted; where Europeans always looked upon the natives as inferior races fit for hewing wood and drawing water; where all senior posts in the civil or other services were clearly designated *European posts*. In some places like Kenya the natives

were actually put on reserves. It is true that these practices of discrimination are now matters of recent history in
most territories; but they could not be expected to be of
good omen for any system of government qualified by the
word *Native*—and so *Native* Administration could not be
trusted.

(vi) Finally, it was suspected in certain quarters that the
Indirect Rule system was merely an imposition resulting
from the apparent quasi-conquest of Northern Nigeria by the
British; otherwise why was it not introduced into the Gold
Coast first, where British contact had been much earlier
than in Nigeria? (British connection with the Gold Coast
started in the seventeenth century, although no legal status
had been given to the coastal trading settlements until the
British Settlements Act was passed in 1843. In 1874 the
Gold Coast Colony was created by Letters Patent and Orders
in Council. The Gold Coast was regarded as made up of
Treaty States whose chiefs, in accordance with their
respective treaties with the British Government, enjoyed a
large measure of independence which could hardly favour
an orthodox practice of Indirect Rule system, and actually
encouraged, until recent reforms, some form of rivalry
between the Government and the ruling chiefs in matters of
local administration.)

Such facts—and others which may have to be mentioned
in the succeeding chapters—formed the background for
the violent distrust of the Indirect Rule System among
nationalists. It is to be admitted that some of the points
mentioned above may in themselves be controversial; but
this does not remove the fact that they did exist, even though
no one might have expressed them in such crystallized forms
as has just been done.

It is, of course, not the intention to defend the points,
or even to pass any judgement in favour or against those
who might have held, or been influenced by, them;
but it is worth suggesting that the important thing for
the present is for all concerned to forget the unpleasant

past or origin of things if to do so would be helpful to progress.

This should not be taken as an inference that one necessarily agrees with the argument that the original intention of Indirect Rule was bad. But granting, for the sake of argument, that it was so, later operators and interpreters of the system have given it different and beneficial meanings. It has, for instance, been seen as a basis for political and social development; or, as Sir Donald Cameron understood it, as a basis for partnership between Britain and the colonies; or even, as Dr. Mair has put it, as 'the progressive adaptation of native institutions to modern conditions'. (*Native Policies in Africa*, p. 56.) Whether the system was introduced as one of choice or of necessity, there is hardly any doubt now that it did materially succeed (or can materially succeed where it is still in practice) along the lines of these later conceptions; and one might even go further and say that if the direct system of administration adopted by the French, or even the Germans in their colonial days, were adopted in, say, Nigeria, political progress might not have been as rapid as it has been. It is permissible to make this unequivocal assertion at this time when the Indirect Rule system is, gradually, running out, and is to be replaced by something more modern and more progressive; and it is only fair that one should give it its full due. Itself unable to grow further or, maybe, too old to continue to weather the storm—in some parts of Africa at least—it is giving birth, maturely it is hoped, to the modern and more progressive systems of local government now coming into being. In no other way can a worthy epitaph for this old system be expressed than in the success of the coming systems.

There would appear to be no better way of composing an epitaph for Indirect Rule at this stage than by giving it a passing examination from the background of such areas as the Eastern Region of Nigeria, where it has been regarded as not being as successful as it has been judged to be in, say, the Northern Region of Nigeria. The reason for taking this risk of boring readers with some repetition of what would appear to be already well-known, lies in our strong conviction that, like Biblical narratives, the story may be old and well-known but the moral will still be new, interesting and useful for the daily tasks ahead.

It is generally agreed, that the main reason for the great success of the system in the Northern Region of Nigeria has been the fact that there were already in existence 'organizations which could be readily adapted as an instrument of local rule' (Hailey), for these indigenous organizations have been the bases on which the Indirect Rule system has been built. These 'ready organizations' had been made possible by an external conquest by the Fulani invaders. It was quite natural that these conquerors, in order to bring the conquered under safe control, should place large areas of the conquered territories under central and unified controls. History shows that this is typical of all conquerors. It is worth noting that the ready material, even in the Northern Region itself, was limited to those parts affected by the Fulani conquest. Hardly anywhere else in Africa, *not affected by similar circumstances*, can organizations similar in extent and solidarity to the Fulani imperial emirates of Nigeria be found.[1] Purely native organizations as a rule are usually less extensive and less solid. The ruling Emirs of Northern Nigeria were virtual autocrats (virtual, because traditionally the Emirs had always had Advisory Councils which they always consulted on all matters of importance; the institution of Sole Native Authorities being one of the offsprings of Indirect Rule), and this had been made possible by the military circumstances of their power. Purely native organizations or systems could hardly welcome or tolerate autocracy in any form, and the reasons for this are not far to seek. Here the chief was one of the people, derived of, and related by blood to them. He could not

[1] The fairly large chiefdoms of the Gold Coast or even of the Western Region of Nigeria are not without significance of a military past.

therefore claim any mysterious or military superiority over those of whom he was head, and was always obliged to consult, and act in accordance with, the people's wishes.

These were fundamental facts which appear to have been almost lost sight of by the early apostles of Indirect Rule carrying its gospel and practice from Northern Nigeria to other parts of Africa. We do not propose, of course, to make a general survey of the system in all aspects—that would be outside the scope of this work, quite apart from other limitations. Rather we shall, if we may repeat ourselves, confine our remarks and observations to the system as practised in less fertile areas of Africa—areas where there were no powerful centralized indigenous authorities. We shall carry out our brief study objectively, in the belief and hope that useful lessons for the future may be drawn from such a study—possibly from the mistakes made. The study will be based on Eastern Nigeria, which may fairly be described as a classical example.

The commonest mistake committed by the early apostles of the Indirect Rule system was the frequently over-hasty assumption that hardly any indigenous authorities worthy of reckoning with existed, wherever they failed to see such institutions as the Emirates of Northern Nigeria. That this was a sad mistake need hardly be stressed for, in the words of Sir Donald Cameron, 'in the various tribal units and sub-units, native society, with a few exceptions, is organized in some manner or another; every man is not a law unto himself'. (*Native Administration in Nigeria and Tanganyika.* Sir Donald gives as examples of the 'few exceptions' the sophisticated cosmopolitan town like Lagos,[1] and the extremely primitive and nomadic people like the *Wandirobo* of Tanganyika, or the pigmies of the Congo who are deeply hidden in the forest.) What was really necessary was patience with hard work to discover the exact native structures of society, with a view to evolving

[1] The mention of Lagos is a little inaccurate, for despite its cosmopolitanism, Lagos has well-recognised traditional authorities.

a means of adapting them to modern requirements, for the purpose of local government or native administration.

The mistake was perhaps first committed in South-Eastern Nigeria, where the early administrators started to make use of the most forward (and sometimes the most rascally) of the natives as agents of administration. There were no, and of course could not be, indigenous southern 'emirs'—as was the case in the Northern part—to be found. The true leaders of the people were not discovered—that is assuming that really serious efforts had been made to discover them. The most forward elements already mentioned were therefore intended to play the role of 'indigenous authorities' but, far from being able to play such a role, they turned out in actual fact to be no less notorious than the German pre-1914 *Akidas* in Tanganyika.[1] They were appointed by warrant and were known as 'warrant chiefs' and expected perhaps to command enough respect from those over whom they were placed—a hope which was later naturally completely dashed. This no doubt was what Sir Donald Cameron in his *Native Administration in Nigeria and Tanganyika* appropriately describes as trying to 'make, as it were, a crown or a king at the top and then try to find something underneath on which it might—perhaps—appropriately be placed', which is what he says he saw in Eastern Nigeria in 1931.

The steps thus taken were, as we have said, a mistake soon to be heavily paid for—in riots and blood. An indigenous chief, as distinct from a conqueror, in Africa could never, as has been seen, be a despot. Many restraining influences surrounded him, the most basic of which were, possibly, religious. He was compelled to order himself strictly in accordance with accepted principles of

[1] The Germans in their days in Tanganyika adopted the Arab method of appointing natives as their agents in carrying out their governmental policy. These agents excessively abused their positions and were very strongly disliked and criticized even by some of the Germans themselves.

custom, tradition and taboos. He generally had a group
of recognized advisers who helped him to rule properly.
Should he abuse his position, his people could easily show
disapproval by rebellion (which might even result in the
death of the chief) or deposition. He had no organized
force (police or army) to keep down his rebellious
subjects.

The position of the newly created 'warrant chiefs' was
the direct reverse of that of the indigenous chief. They
owed their position not to tradition or to the general wish of
those over whom they were placed, but to an external
authority, generally suspicious of indigenous and traditional
practices as possibly barbarous and repugnant if not
inhuman, and having the means, the police and the army,
to enforce its wish or keep down rebellion. The new 'chiefs'
were therefore not only free from traditional inhibitions but
adequately strengthened and protected and could do anything that suited them, no matter how offensive and objec-
tionable it was to custom and tradition, provided it did not
offend, or come to the notice of, the authority to whom they
owed their positions. As in all cases where power and
authority are suddenly thrust into the hands of those who
are fully conscious that they have no right to such power
and authority, or are not qualified or good enough to
exercise them, these 'chiefs' straight away abused their
positions. One result of such extensive abuse of power on
the part of these 'warrant chiefs' was the Women's Riots of
1929 in Eastern Nigeria.

These riots, amongst other things, directly or indirectly
emphasized the importance of traditional authorities, a fact
clearly acknowledged by the Commission of Enquiry into
the riots. Their immediate cause was the rumour that
women, like their male counterparts who had started to be
taxed two years before in 1927, were going to be taxed. But
it was substantially more a revolt against those upstarts,
the 'warrant chiefs', rather than against the Government as
such. Nobody could trust those 'artificial chiefs' whose

35

misdeeds and rascality had already earned them deserved general unpopularity and dislike. There is no doubt that the women had active support of men who in some cases actually disguised themselves as women and joined in the widespread acts of violence, under the misguided, but soon discredited belief, that the white man was a worshipper of women and so would not shoot them! Had the Government discovered and recognized the traditional chiefs and leaders of the people the unfortunate episode might, at least, not have taken so serious a turn as it eventually did. There are some of those displaced leaders in that part of the world to-day who can reliably confirm this statement.

Now, the absence of strong centralized powerful authorities in the Eastern Region of Nigeria does not mean that the people live a life of beasts, without any organized social system, law and control—apart from what the central government is now giving them. They have never been communities where everybody is 'a law unto himself'. They are a naturally democratic people, but even democracy is based on one kind of tradition or another. They have indigenous ways of controlling and ordering the modes of their lives. They have authorities which they recognize and respect among themselves. What they do not have are virtual autocrats lording it over those they rule. The people by their nature value individual liberties and so cannot place too much power in the hands of individuals. Their political heads might be loosely described as 'constitutional' heads in whose names the respective villages are governed in the native way. Among such 'constitutional' heads may be numbered the *Obong of Calabar*, the *Ntoes of the Quas*, the *Nkukus* (now *Mbong Ikpa Isong* about whom more later) of Ibibio people, the *Obis* or *Igwes*, etc., of Ibo people. All these people are the greatly adored heads of their people but they do not in their own persons rule the people. They always have what may be rightly likened to a sort of 'Councils of Ministers' who are the real law makers and

36

executors, without whom or whose advice the 'constitutional' heads can do nothing. Under these 'constitutional' heads, in the individual villages, are age-grades of various types specializing in, or rather charged with, specific responsibilities in the villages. One age-grade may see to the roads, another to the markets and so on. In addition they check and rule the proper conduct of their individual members. Examples of such age-grades are the *Ndichies, Umudiabas, Otukpokolos*, and various *Nkas* of Ibibioland, etc., found in some areas of the Region. This age-grade system is more common among the Ibos than among their brothers the Ibibios, and in some areas these age-grades are the real 'local authorities' in the villages.

Unfortunately there has been a long and deep-rooted belief in certain quarters that these traditional authorities constituted no powerful or useful influences, or merely represented something tied to primitive, undesirable and superstitious beliefs. A casual visitor is most likely to leave that part of Nigeria with that erroneous belief. The reasons for this are simple: many official reports, particularly the earliest ones, give that impression, and in schools run by Christian Missions (and most schools are) children are, understandably, taught to abhor anything connected with these organizations, with the result that the majority of educated people, even after they are grown up, are deplorably ignorant of exactly what some of their native societies and organizations stand for; and have come to regard association with these societies or organizations, as something incompatible with their education. That is why one is easily apt to meet with educated and influential Africans who will readily say that these societies or organizations are bad and undesirable, and that the sooner they are done away with the better; and this because they have not taken the trouble to appraise impartially the real merits of these societies. Of course, their general indifference or disapproval has never succeeded in killing these organizations, because in any African society the educated people are always in the minority.

That some of these societies were usually connected with things repugnant to civilized (i.e. modern) or Christian ethics, particularly in the methods of enforcing their orders, is undeniable; that their influences are waning fast and may ultimately disappear is admissible; but that they can be destroyed with a wave of the hand is doubtful. They are native institutions, and it is possible to wonder if it might not have been a wiser policy for the educated members of society to have gone into these organizations and from the inside develop them into modern institutions acceptable to modern standards and requirements. As already remarked, these institutions are dying hard, and it would be difficult for one to agree that their influences in the villages have disappeared altogether or can easily do so in the near future. They have merely been drastically modified, reduced or driven underground by modern influences of politics and religion. Offences which used to be punished in the 'traditional way' are now punished in native courts, and it is significant to remark that very often, where it is an offence against custom or village law, the prosecutors are usually representatives of the particular age-grade in whose field of special responsibility the offence might have been committed.

A local government system, in a place such as the one we have been considering, can afford to ignore these indigenous authorities at, say, the District or County levels, but it is extremely doubtful if it can with advantage do so at *village* levels. We shall return to this later; meanwhile the moral of the 1929 riots remains.

After the riots, the Government was brought face to face with realities; but it was perhaps a little too late. The harm had been done; and the work or success of the fairly real native authorities of later years was in some ways to be hampered by the deep-rooted suspicion engendered by the behaviour of the original 'warrant chiefs', behaviour which had been directly or indirectly responsible for the riots which had cost husbands their wives and children their mothers.

Writing ten years later (in 1937) Sir Donald Cameron, if one may quote him again, had these striking and true remarks to make of the original position in the Eastern Region of Nigeria:

> In the Southern Nigeria in the old days when the primary consideration was to open up the country that trade and revenue might follow and allow the new dependency to be self-supporting, the Calabar Government did not think of finding the real leaders of the people—perhaps they had no time for that kind of thing—and used as their medium for intercourse with the people the loudest-mouthed ruffian that presented himself to their notice. As a result of this policy little was done in the way of Native Administration among the large tribes such as the Ibo and the Ibibio, nothing of value, indeed, until the last few years.

The something of 'value' of later years was the more earnest attempt, encouraged by Sir Donald himself, to find 'the real leaders of the people'.

These were found, but, as has been seen, their spheres of influence were often too small and limited—so much so that they could not individually be used as a basis for local government or administration. Small units had therefore to be grouped together under common native courts (and later common native treasuries), care being taken to ensure that each area was represented by leaders acceptable to the people. Where these representatives resulted in too large numbers, these were broken down into two or more panels sitting in turn.

The new bodies grew in importance and responsibility and after some years of experience, it was possible to amalgamate them still further into larger authorities with much stronger finances. The ease and success with which this was done in certain areas provided encouragement for the Government to make the federation of native authorities and treasuries into larger and stronger units a definite policy, thus preparing grounds for the introduction of the advanced local government reforms which have been taking place in Eastern Region since 1950.

In the Ibibio area in particular these amalgamations were very happily welcomed by the Ibibio State Union, a cultural and welfare organization of the people, which at once decided to provide some unifying symbols, permanent and generally recognized and respected by the people, to these enlarged clans. Accordingly at its annual conference of 1948, or thereabout, it decided to institute the offices of Clan Heads (*Mbong Ikpa Isong*). These offices were to be occupied by fairly progressive leaders selected and recognized by the people as such. These new offices were to be symbols of unity, responsible to the people and the Union, purely honorary[1] and without any religious or other sectional ties attached to them. Any suitable leader of the people, Christian and non-Christian, was to be eligible to it. This step was taken because it was felt that the purely traditional leaders, the *Nkukus*, who were generally the oldest men in the clans and forbidden by religious and traditional taboos to move about freely, or even to go out at all on certain days of the week, were not suitable for the modern needs of fast developing communities. The proposals were most enthusiastically welcomed by all sections of the communities involved. The new Clan Heads were elected in the traditional way and installed with expensive pomp and pageantry, the cost being borne by contributions from men and women of the clans concerned. The Native Authorities gave them recognition, but this was virtually negatived by the Central Government which, with its usual and understandable caution, refused to give official recognition to these Clan Heads and consequently refused to approve any financial provisions for some allowances for

---

[1] It is possible that, if these Clan Heads were properly used in local government administration, some allowances or honoraria would, fairly, be claimed for them.

them inserted in some of the Native Treasury Estimates by the Native Authorities concerned. These Clan Heads, no less than the people concerned, are now completely embarrassed, particularly as, in some cases, the modern local government bodies do not seem to take any notice of them. It may here be added that, in nine cases out of ten, these Clan Heads were amongst the most important personalities in the old Native Administration Councils. The writer is one of those who very deeply regret the present position of these Clan Heads, and it is at present difficult to assess what damage has been done, not only to the cause of unity in the respective clans, but to the cause of the new local government bodies as well, as a result of their apparently frustrated positions.

We must return to the Native Authorities. After the federations, and until the introduction of the new local government reforms into some areas, the day to day administration of local affairs continued to fall entirely upon the shoulders of the District Officers, with the Native Authorities playing the role of what might appropriately be described as Advisory Bodies. While some Native Authorities, which contained some educated elements, were fairly capable of playing their part satisfactorily, others were not so good. In the former case the District Officer always found it a help and of use to consult them as much and often as possible; but in the latter it was often a sheer waste of time to consult them at all and during times of acute staff shortage the District Officers were very often compelled into the *justified* practice of doing what needed doing without consultation and telling the Native Authorities afterwards, and sometimes 'forgetting to tell them afterwards'. As can be understood, this latter case was what people were prone to notice and criticize, rather than the former—hence the all-too-frequent unkind and sharp criticism of the officers concerned. It would be wrong to think that the District Officers enjoyed acting alone, for they themselves regarded it as an undesirable necessity; and that is why most of them desired reforms as much as any other person. Estimates and major expenditures were always discussed with the Councils—whether bad or good councils—before action was taken, and this was one case in which the District Officer would never act 'and tell the people afterwards or forget to tell them afterwards'.

The practice just briefly described was quite different from what usually obtained in the areas with strong native authorities—parts of the North or West Regions of Nigeria for instance—where the Indirect Rule system could be orthodoxly practised. Here the practice was for the District Officers to keep themselves always in the background, from which they could advise or persuade the Chiefs on what to do in respect of local administration. In actual practice the Chiefs themselves always sought and received such advice. It is true that in some cases such advice had the force of instruction from the District Officer or the Resident. It is equally true to say that under the Indirect Rule system as a whole, no matter where practised or whether the District Officer remained in the background or in the forefront, the final word rested with the central government through Administrative Officers. The appointment[1] of Native Authorities was vested in the Governor who was usually advised by Administrative Officers on the spot; the Annual Estimates of the Authorities, and actual expenditure of the funds provided therein, were subject to control by the central government. Someone indeed who has described the system as government by the Central Authority *through* indigenous authorities did not very much miss the mark, and of course, that is what the term 'warrant' implies!

As hinted at the beginning of this chapter the Indirect Rule system has been subject to much adverse criticism. This criticism was not always really justified, being often unkind and misinformed, or just based on the common but misleading practice of judging the present by the past.

[1] These appointments were usually made by warrant.

Indirect Rule had many shortcomings and disadvantages, as indeed anything devised or operated by man must have; but these, it is not impossible to say, were adequately offset by its successes and advantages. It was often branded as being too conservative and unprogressive, but we have earlier seen how it showed itself surprisingly adaptable to change when it voluntarily opened its doors to educated members in order to meet advanced constitutional requirements.

Those who could not blame the system as such, blamed those who served as its organs—the Chiefs—as ignorant and unprogressive. While this was true of the Chiefs in many cases, it could not rightly be said to be a general rule. There is evidence to show that the Chiefs, armed with long experience, very often exhibited a greater degree of realism and responsibility than their younger educated colleagues in the Councils. Some years ago, for instance, in a certain place in Nigeria, a rate was to be introduced by the Native Authority to meet local services. The younger educated councillors wished to levy a general flat rate on men and women in the area. The Head Chief (who was also the head of the N.A. Council), while agreeing in principle that women should rightly make some contribution towards the provision of local services, did not favour a general flat rate on men and women alike, and urged instead rates on tenements, which in effect would mean women of property paying as well as men. It was not a question of the Chief being so 'unprogressive' as to feel that women should not pay rates, but a question of commonsense, tact and method. He was overruled by majority vote of the Council, but later events proved that the course he had advised was the right one in the circumstances.

Let the new reforms, which will inevitably (radically in some cases) change the position of the traditional elders and chiefs be pursued with vigour and determination; but do not let sight be lost completely of the traditional chiefs and what they represent. For, as Dr. Mair says in *Native*

Administration in Central Nyasaland, 'if hereditary (i.e. traditional) rulers are in fact the "real repositories" of authority
they will continue to be so, even if local government passes
into other hands'.   If by law you can take away powers
from traditional authorities, who in fact may be the 'real
repositories of authority' among the people, you cannot by
the same means take away the affectionate place and respect
which their positions might have engendered in the people's
hearts.   This means that although by law you can stop
them from exercising their traditional authority, you cannot
by law maintain the very moderating influences which their
positions alone could make possible in societies.   Unfortunately this fact is seldom (if ever) appreciated until there
is local trouble and the people get out of hand and there is
no effective local restraint.   Perhaps here may lie, at least
a partial explanation, of why women and children could
leave their husbands' and parents' homes to oppose with
violence measures of development introduced by the new
constituted authorities? It is heartening to note, as hinted
in the previous chapter, that in certain parts of Africa the
tendency is to make these offices of Chief constitutional
ones.

There was one strongly dreaded risk in the old system—
the risk of creating an oligarchy of ruling classes from among
the traditional authorities.   This risk was appreciated under
the Indirect Rule system, and has since then been successfully guarded against if not destroyed.   It is equally
important for the future to ensure that the avoidance of the
risk in one direction does not mean transferring it to another
—from the traditional rulers to a section of the rising middle
classes.

In Africa it is customary for children to erect monuments,
on which adequate epitaphs are inscribed, to their deceased
mothers.   The old mother of local government systems in
Africa, whose children are now ready to take her place,
is passing away; and we suggest to the new local government bodies, her children, the following—perhaps badly

composed—epitaph for their ailing mother whose days are but numbered:

> Our Old Mother Indirect Rule
> Liked, Disliked and Misunderstood;
> Thou Didst Play Thy Part Well,
> Laying Solid Foundations For Days Ahead;
> We Shall Not Forget Thee Whate'er We Do.

CHAPTER III

WHAT IS LOCAL GOVERNMENT?

IN early days, in Africa as anywhere else in the world, government—that is whatever there was of it—had been mainly concerned with the maintenance of law and order. This, in primitive societies, also involved protection of local inhabitants against attacks, murder and brigandage from neighbouring equally primitive and wild societies. (The main preoccupation of European Administrative Officers in Africa, performing the functions of local administration, was the maintenance of law and order in the widest sense of the expression.) Once societies become civilized, stabilized and law-abiding the functions of local government must needs extend beyond the province of mere maintenance of law and order; and in modern times, where the all-embracing State is well organized and efficient, maintenance of law and order is becoming relatively a secondary function of local authorities as such. The principal interest of local government now lies essentially in the provision of human needs—spiritual, material and social—for the people; in education, health and general happiness and comfort for the people. To do this effectively it has become imperative that the people concerned, who require these services or for whom they are to be provided, must themselves be made to participate more fully and actively in their provision. They must be able to decide, or help to influence decision on, what is good for them, and be prepared to undertake and shoulder responsibilities both in cost and administration of such services. That is why we are now having the modern forms of local government in Africa in succession to the old forms of native administration the machineries of which, while fully useful and acceptable in their own days, have become too old and out-of-date for modern needs.

It has been pointed out in an earlier chapter that the fact that the old nomenclature of 'Native Administration' is being replaced by a more acceptable, though hardly very clarifying, term of 'Local Government' does not mean that there have hitherto been no local government systems at all in African territories. They had always existed in one form or another, with different aims and ends perhaps, even before the introduction of European administration into some parts of Africa. Before the *Europeans* they might have been unorganized, unsystematic and inefficient; primitive and sometimes bloody; despotic and enslaving, and so on. With the advent of Europeans the forms might be said to have been more organized and systematic, more efficient and utilitarian; but they have necessarily still remained different and varied from place to place.

It is extremely difficult to find a comprehensive or even a generally acceptable definition of 'local government', which may vary in aims and patterns from one country or area to another; may take entirely different forms in non-self-governing countries from what exists in self-governing ones; may *anywhere* take forms varying from entrusting the actual day-to-day administration of the areas into the hands of popularly elected councillors, to ones in which such administration is left in the hands of single individuals appointed by, and responsible to, either the central government or the elected councils; from a system of 'partnership' between the central government and locally elected council, to one in which the local bodies act as mere agents of the central or state governments, and so on and so forth. All these systems exist in the world to-day.

We have inferred above that the term 'local government' is not a very clarifying one, in other words, may well be misleading. It is often made much more so by the addition of so pretentious a word as *self*—thus we often see or hear people talk of 'local *self*-government'. Let us examine this statement in the light of what an eminent and famous authority has said.

47

EPITAPH TO INDIRECT RULE

Sir Ivor Jennings in his *Principles of Local Government Law* states, in his definition of the term, that since it is 'government', the systems of local government which a country develops must be part of its governmental or constitutional structure; and since it is 'local' it relates to specific portions of the country defined by locality.

Now the word *government*. 'Government' can be defined as implying the idea of authoritative administration or some exercise of authority that is at once effective and continuous; also 'the exercise of knowledge and judgement as well as power'. If we add the word *self*, as is very often done, it will also imply the idea of autonomy free from external control. The explanation of 'government', *but without 'self'*, as we have just seen, might be acceptable in the context 'local government' if the word *power* were qualified to show that such power as a local government body may have is always given to it by the Central Government. But if by the addition of the word *self* it implies an idea of autonomy free from external control, the term can at once be disqualified, for it would then be false. If there could be—as there certainly was—'local self-government' in past ages when societies were less complex and complicated, and social needs much more simple as well as less taxing and demanding, it cannot be so now, and never will, unless the human race is prepared to retrace its steps along the path of progress which it is now treading fast—and this notwithstanding the arguments advanced by some scholarly writers that local government bodies could regain their independence from central government control by the introductions of what they call local income tax by or for local authorities. (This, however, is not the place to pursue the point.) Again if, as Sir Ivor says, a system of local government which a country develops must be part of its governmental or constitutional structure, it is doubtful how there can be truly *self-governing* local authorities free from central government control.

At the risk of being a little pedantic, it is here necessary to make passing remarks on this question of local government being a part of governmental or constitutional structure of the country in which it is operated; for it is a conception which was almost disastrously misunderstood some years ago in Africa by some national leaders who felt, rather honestly, that local government reforms should await the attainment of national self-government, for it would be then that the governmental and constitutional structures of the different dependent nations could be known. It is fairly true to say that it is now generally agreed, on the contrary, that early and proper practice in local government is the surest foundation for national political responsibility. Constitutional or governmental structure of a country affects her local government institutions only generally and on principle—in so far as the country concerned is democratic or totalitarian, stable or unstable. A democratic and stable country cannot be afraid of local government bodies to which it is prepared to allow a free hand in the conduct and management of their own affairs. A totalitarian or unstable government on the other hand cannot afford the luxury of allowing its local government bodies a great degree of independence. Hitler, for instance, on his march to dictatorship, started by depriving local government bodies of any effective independence. No territory in Africa, it is hoped, anticipates any totalitarian status, and so the form that our local government systems should take may be said to be fairly clear and assured. There is no need therefore to delay, and the necessary reforms can proceed even where national self-government is not in sight!

Now the word *local*, which Sir Ivor takes to signify specific portions of the country defined by locality. This cannot be said to be completely free from ambiguity. In countries with federal Constitutions—the United States, Canada, Australia and, for that matter, Nigeria—there are States or Regions which are specific portions defined by locality, but whose governments are not *local government*. 'Local', in our opinion, should be defined to imply a sense of 'community feeling', which is another way of saying that the different units should more or less comprise people of similar outlook, common needs and problems and (where they exist) common or similar customs and tradition. (It must be here acknowledged that in purely artificial, or even highly cosmopolitan towns, the most that can be expected of the inhabitants are common needs and problems arising from their happening to belong to a common community of persons, and hardly any of the other qualities.) It should also imply that the units are so compact and so intimately connected with each other that no elected member should feel, or be regarded as, a 'stranger' in the councils. There is yet another precaution that must be taken against the use of the word *local*. There are certain statutory boards— e.g. electricity boards, marketing boards, coal boards, etc.— which serve specific portions of a country but which are not local government bodies.

Yet, one cannot confidently suggest that the term 'local government' should be abandoned. It is a favourite term which must stay so long as one understands it in the proper sense. And here let us try to give a definition of the term as we understand it.

By 'local government' is meant the breaking down of a country into small units or localities for the purpose of ADMINISTRA-TION, in which the inhabitants of the different units or localities concerned play a direct and full part through their elected representatives, who exercise powers or undertake functions under the general authority of the National Government.

The definition may perhaps appear clumsy, but it should be sufficient for our purpose. It will be seen that we have used the word *administration*, instead of *government*, in the above definition. That is because it is felt to be a better word for the context. The fact that all functions of local government bodies are given to them by the central government; the fact that they have no legislative powers in their own right; and the fact that in some cases they more or less act as agents of central government (e.g. in the United

Kingdom when they collect vehicle licence fees, carry out Government building programmes, etc.) make them more administrative than governmental bodies.

In the definition mention has been made of the breaking down of a country into smaller units or localities for the purpose of local government. This leads to the question of size, and later to the organization, of the units. The size of the units must needs vary from country to country, or even from place to place within the same country. It will all depend on what are the aims and purpose of local government. In the colonies these aims and purposes have been well defined as has been seen in previous chapters—the training of local people for higher political responsibilities and the provision of social services. Both of these two aims are irreproachable ones. In Britain, for example, some of the best and most prominent members of Parliament—statesmen and not just ordinary politicians—graduated from services in local government bodies which gave them sound foundation and training; and so to regard local government in Africa as a means of training for national responsibility and leadership is not peculiar. In the same way, local government would have no meaning or even appeal if it did not carry with it the responsibility for provision of social services. If these two aims then must be achieved properly, it does appear that two considerations must influence the size of the local government bodies, namely:

(1) The units of administration must be large enough to take in reasonable essential social services.

(2) The units must at the same time be small enough to be able to arouse and sustain the interest and civic pride of the local inhabitants and electors.

What are *reasonable essential services* will, like anything else about local government, vary between different places and countries. We shall pursue this point in greater detail in a subsequent chapter when we come to discuss responsibilities and functions of local government bodies; but we might here remark that it would be dangerous to allow the provision of essential services to overshadow all else. There will certainly be some essential services which cannot, for reasons of economy and convenience, be provided within one local government area. It would be wrong in any case to base the size of local government units on technical and engineering requirements—on what would be an ideal area, from a technical and economic point of view, for the provision of electricity, water, construction of roads and so on.

Fortunately, in African colonial territories (of Britain) such an essential service as electricity, where provided, is the responsibility not of local government bodies but of central government or public corporations. But what if in some parts it should be decided that the electricity supply should be the responsibility of local government bodies, merely because a group of enthusiasts with enough influence have seen that such is the practice in another part of the world? A local government body capable of doing this economically would be very large indeed. For instance, in the Eastern Region of Nigeria it is considered that it would be most economical to generate electricity from two most advantageous sources, the Kwa Falls in the Calabar Province and Oji River in Onitsha Province, to serve most of the Region. If this were to be undertaken by single local government bodies it would mean having two County Council areas which would be larger than some state government areas of certain countries. This, of course, is only a hypothetical illustration since the electricity supply is not the responsibility of local government bodies in that part of the world. But the water supply will most likely be their responsibility; and as demand increases with the opening up and development of rural areas, it will be found that it will be more economical to supply it from vantage points which may necessarily have to transcend the boundaries of more than one local government body; otherwise it will be necessary to have over-large units which will totally defeat the second consideration mentioned above.

It has been said that local government elections to the County Councils are usually dull and unexciting because the administrative areas of the County Councils are usually too large to arouse really local interest in their activities. This is true not only of British Counties but of Counties in the African territories, where modern local government has been introduced, and follows the British pattern. If the aim of using local government as a basis of training in political responsibility is not to be defeated, steps should be taken to see that the areas of the local government units are not so extensive as to make them cease to be really *local*. And this brings us to the question of organization.

In some colonial territories the tendency in modernizing local government systems has been to borrow or adopt something of the British system of organization. To a visitor to Britain, who is interested in local government, the British method of organization is bound to appear confusing, anomalous and almost without any perceptible logic. His confusion becomes all the more increased when he sees in this small country six different kinds of local government bodies—the Administrative County, the County Borough, the Non-County Borough, the Urban District Council, the Rural District Council, and the Parish Council. If he is patient enough to do some 'sorting out' he may be able to reduce the different types into four different groups of Administrative County, County Borough, County District (under which head will come the Non-County Borough, Urban District Council, and the Rural District Council, all of which perform fairly similar functions, have similar administrative status; but for reasons of geography or history, may enjoy different civic or ceremonial privileges), and lastly the Parish. But, at least as regards the first three categories of local government bodies named in the above classification, he will still find himself confronted with astounding disparities in size, population and resources even among the authorities of the same type and status. Among the County types he will find at one extreme

53

the largest County with a population of 2,270,000 and at the other extreme the smallest with only 18,000; among the County Borough types, the largest with a population of 1,085,000 and the smallest with 25,000; and among the County District types the largest Urban District Council with a population of 200,000 and the smallest with only 700, with 1d. rate products of £8,600 and £16 respectively. The figures, taken from the Report of the Local Government Boundary Commission for the year 1947, do not include the County of London which occupies a special position.

For some time past, and most strongly since the Second World War, there has been a general feeling that the present arrangements, which date from over seventy years ago, need drastic and urgent reform. But any Government bold enough to carry out the reforms is bound to incur a good deal of unpopularity from one section or another, which may even affect its chances at a general election, for opinion is sharply divided. Since arriving in the United Kingdom, where these lines are being written, the writer has had the privilege of reading a good deal of literature by all interested sections of the country, on this question of reform. Unfortunately, running through most of this vast amount of literature, some form of partisan feeling can be seen, political and otherwise, inclining the authors one way or the other, which cannot help the various recommendations to earn any degree of general acceptability; and this is no less true of books written by eminent authorities such as University professors. Recently the writer also had the privilege of listening to a lively debate between representatives of two opposing factions—one favouring drastic reform of the present system and the creation of one-tier all-purpose authorities to replace the present Counties and County Districts, and the other favouring the maintenance of the *status quo* with some modifications. Interesting and informative as the arguments adduced were, an unprejudiced listener could not help coming to the justified conclusion that the speakers were simply trying to defend the system they knew best or were, for some reason or other, in duty bound to defend. In other words, they were merely, so it appeared to the writer at least, expressing 'their masters' voices' as was clearly evidenced by their repeated practice of giving answers to any question from the audience by simply quoting relevant extracts from booklets prepared by their different associations. There was hardly any sign of pursuing the question objectively, nor readiness to appreciate the other man's point of view, nor willingness to compromise. (Indeed in one of the booklets, so freely quoted from by the debaters, it is clearly laid down by one of the contending parties that, in view of the amount of work and thought put into the preparation of their memorandum, they were not prepared to accept any alteration in their plans!) No wonder then that the task for reform has been so difficult. Both, however, agreed that the present system needed reform, and that was useful enough for an outsider like the writer, who made a lot of deductions from their arguments.

Far from trying to be unduly critical, we have brought out the above points to show two things: Firstly, the inadvisability of trying to copy too much of the English system at a time when everybody seems agreed that the system needs substantial reforms. Secondly, *the difficulty of carrying out reforms after any particular system has taken deep roots.* This second point is of considerable importance, for it points to the need, in the new territories, for taking a long term view in whatever systems or patterns are being evolved.

There is now the question of organization.

Subject to necessary changes and modifications to be dictated by local needs and circumstances, it might be considered much more preferable to base *the new systems in Africa on two-tier patterns of Village and District, with coordinating agencies in place of Counties, which would take over the*

55

management, provision, and control of those services which may be too large, too expensive, or too uneconomical to be provided at the District Council levels. How the Co-ordinating Authorities should be constituted or staffed, and what functions they should be responsible for, we shall indicate or suggest in subsequent chapters. Meanwhile it is better to try here to defend, if we can, this rather strange suggestion.

Any County Council area, if the Council is to live up to its name and responsibilities (at least as understood in Britain) must necessarily be so large, particularly in African territories where resources on the whole are much more limited and sparse, as to cease to be really local in character. It would accordingly be too remote to be able to arouse and sustain political interest and civic pride, *vis-à-vis* its activities, among the ordinary citizens. Being so remote the Council would not have that desirable close contact with those it serves, so as to be able to know their real needs and their ability to meet those needs. In consequence of this the Council might be tempted, through ignorance, to provide services which the people cannot honestly afford to pay for, or as somebody has put it, 'try to provide luxuries for those who cannot afford necessities'. Even if it managed to guard against this last temptation, its mere existence might tempt the national government to try to give it too heavy responsibilities for which the rate-payers might not be able to provide the necessary funds.

A further point is that the cost in staff, building, etc., for many County Councils lead to an unduly heavy financial burden on the rate-payer who has also to provide for the needs of the Village and District Councils—expensive duplications in territories as yet financially too poor to indulge in such luxuries.

Lastly, in any of the territories, the number of men and women capable of serving usefully and intelligently on the councils is as yet too limited to be able to meet the requirements of too many councils. All these and other considerations favour the establishment of Co-ordinating

Agencies which would take over the work, perhaps, of more than one county.

We make no pretence that the above reasons are entirely defensible against any person who really proposes to attack them. His obvious first point of attack would be the argument that by suggesting that Counties as such should be replaced by Co-ordinating Agencies we are merely trying to call a spade a shovel and nothing more, since the so-called Co-ordinating Agencies would still have to be housed, staffed and in any case precept on the District Councils as Counties do at present. It is possible to accept some truth in this argument—but only to a point.

We would maintain that the Co-ordinating Agency system (which could be given any name) would not be as expensive as the present Counties. In the first place it would be a sort of joint planning or administrative body on which several local authorities, rich and poor, would be represented through elected, appointed or even nominated representatives, according to the choice of each local authority, or as provided by law. Such representatives would be persons best suited for their responsibilities. The Agency would cover larger areas than the present Counties cover individually, and would embrace more authorities. The question of remoteness would not seriously arise since it would be responsible for such services as would be of *general*, as opposed to *specifically local*, interest to the various sections represented on it.

It is expected that the Agency would be financed by the various authorities represented on it according to the relative financial *abilities* of such authorities, which means that the burden or incidence of cost would be more fairly and more lightly spread among the various communities, rich and poor, under the jurisdiction of such Agency, than can be the case with different autonomous and independent Counties doing bits of the same thing in their own ways. Apart from sharing the cost in this way, the provision of such services, as we have in mind, by the suggested Agency would be more economical and efficient, which in turn would have favourable effect on financial burdens to be borne by the rate or tax-payers.

There would be financial savings too from expenditure on staff salaries. Take, for instance, an Agency taking over the functions of say three County Councils. It would not be necessary for it to employ a staff as large as the total employed by the three Counties. Provided the staff is well selected there is no reason why it could not do with a staff equivalent in size to, though perhaps different in status from, that employed by just one County. (We have mentioned difference in status because it must be assumed that the highest executive officers, with their additional qualifications and responsibility, will earn higher remunerations than their counterparts in the County Councils.) In the same way, too, expenditure would be lessened by the very sharp reductions in the number of councillors which would be necessary. There would also be savings in accommodation cost (offices, staff houses, etc.) since only one headquarters would be necessary instead of three.

The above points briefly answer the objections—and many more answers would not be difficult to find. If the new local government bodies must progress satisfactorily, every device at economy and efficiency must be considered; anything that would save the high administrative costs now experienced in some of the new Councils in Nigeria, for instance. We can illustrate this by a concrete example. In one county there are the following administrative machines: a County Council, an Urban District Council, and three (or is it four?) Rural District Councils; each with large staffs and highly paid executive officers, expensive office buildings and staff accommodation, etc., not to mention the many councillors who must at least draw travelling allowances. All these add up to very considerable expenditure out of the extremely meagre resources of the Councils, leaving negligible and completely inadequate margins for the essential services. Apart from perhaps bringing political education and responsibility home to as many people as possible—an assumption not without some misgivings—one cannot help thinking that the huge and duplicated expenditure can hardly be well justified; and this particularly when one realizes that the functions now undertaken by the five or six administrative machines were previously being undertaken, with perhaps slightly higher efficiency, by one or two officials—the D.O. and A.D.O. who had other central government functions to perform in addition—assisted by about one-sixth of the present staff of the joint authorities.

Far from trying to advocate or even justify a return to the old system—which we would be the first to oppose—we have brought out the above concrete facts to show how easy and desirable it is to effect economies in the administration of the new councils.

Before passing on to something else, it is useful to say here that the Co-ordinating Agencies, such as we have suggested, must be really efficient and effective, otherwise there would be no use having them at all. They must not be just loose associations of the various local authorities concerned, but something permanent and with authority. Their staff must be of the highest calibre and hardly inferior to their counterparts in other services. They must be such bodies as would not only be respected, but liked and admired by the lower authorities, and between the two types of authorities there must be free intercourse, mutual respect and confidence.

How do the large towns fit in with our picture? Any move towards the creation of all-purpose authorities based on towns—the counterparts of County Boroughs in England, for example—should be taken with the greatest restraint. In Nigeria, for instance, we would consider it highly desirable that places like Lagos, Ibadan, Kaduna and Enugu, for the simple reasons of their occupying unique positions as seats of central governments, be given this status—the position of Lagos indeed like that of London is already peculiar. There might be one or two other towns, fairly artificial towns built and developed from national funds, such as Port Harcourt, which might also have special claims to this privilege. Beyond this one would be most reluctant to suggest many more. We must learn from English experience and mistakes, which have been most eloquently underlined by unforeseen developments that have taken place since the creation of many County Boroughs. The early creation of many County Boroughs has been one chief cause of the existing anomalies and present friction, which have for so long stood in the way of desirable reforms.

All towns which fulfil certain conditions might be just Urban District Councils, equal counterparts of Rural District Councils. Being urban, they might have special responsibilities arising from their urban position which would not be necessary or appropriate for their rural counterparts. But like the latter, they must come within the jurisdiction of the Co-ordinating Agencies just suggested, or even County Councils where preferred.

In making these proposals we have been influenced by at least three considerations:

(1) Being just urban district councils, and under the jurisdiction of a higher authority in common with their rural neighbours, the future growth or expansion of these towns would be simplified, much more than if they had been autonomous all-purpose authorities. English experience has shown that rural districts, with good reason, always jealously guard against or resist any attempt to 'trespass' into their territories by overgrowing all-purpose authorities with whom they have nothing in common.

(2) All townships derive their revenue largely from the neighbouring rural districts, whose inhabitants sell in, and buy from, the towns. It is also the rural areas which supply food to the towns, and a good proportion of rateable property in these towns is owned by natives or inhabitants of rural areas. It is only fair, in the interest of all concerned,

that the towns should contribute to the development of the rural areas through their common membership to a larger body such as the Co-ordinating Agencies we have advocated.

(3) With increased town planning schemes, community development projects, and industrial expansion, new towns now undreamt of are bound to grow up in years to come; and unless necessary safeguards are now provided, future generations will find themselves confronted with wholesale or incessant demands by these new towns to break away and gain independence from rural connection. It would be difficult if not impossible to resist such demands if reckless precedents are created now. Should such demands be then made many difficult problems will present themselves, one of which will be that what may be left of the rural areas will simply not be able to work.

Our arguments must not, of course, be taken to mean that under no circumstances must a town be given independent status outside a County (or Co-ordinating Agency) organization. To every rule there must be an exception. There may be towns whose populations have grown to figures with which it would be unfair not to give them independent status outside a larger body. One would suggest that a town whose population reached, say, 30,000 (or a little less) and enjoying adequate revenue should be entitled to independent status. It will, however, be some time before many towns in Africa reach this figure, but it is important to bear the fact in mind always.[1]

If anyone should want further arguments before being convinced, one can only advise him to go and study, say, the English experience, which would provide him with enough lessons.[2]

---

[1] In America, however, there are cities whose population far exceeds the population of all the rest of the State put together which enjoy no independent status from the State.

[2] 'Ever since 1888 conflict between counties and county boroughs over boundary extensions and the creation of county boroughs has been a constant feature of local government. These difficulties have been mainly created by growth of population, changes in its distribution

Perhaps we would be expected by readers to suggest sizes for the proposed units in our suggested organization. This, we must confess, would be extremely difficult to do. No general principles can be usefully laid down. All would depend, like anything else discussed in this book, on local circumstances and needs—on the purpose, responsibilities and financial requirements and abilities of the intended authorities. In Nigeria (from where our illustrations will frequently be drawn), for instance, one would suggest two or three Rural District Councils, with one Urban District Council where applicable, to cover one of the largest Administrative Divisions known in that country— it would, of course, be less in smaller Divisions. Our Co-ordinating Agency would cover one of the largest Administrative Divisions and two or more of the smaller ones. For Provinces with good communications, such as Calabar and Onitsha Provinces, we would suggest two Co-ordinating Agencies for the latter and three for the former. These suggestions are, of course, mainly tentative and only intended as an illustration or explanation of what we have in mind.

Now to the Village Councils. Many villages in Africa (in Nigeria certainly) are what would not unjustifiably be described as extended families. For effective local government work and political training, there may be some wisdom in certain cases in amalgamating the existing Village Councils into larger ones, taking into account the close connections of these villages—a group of villages generally shares one market, one church or one school, and this may well provide a basis for amalgamation into larger Village

---

following movements of industry, the growth of urban at the expense of rural population and other circumstances over which local authorities have had little or no control. *The existence of autonomous and ever-growing county boroughs made conflict inevitable. . . .*' (Italics ours.) (*Report of the Local Government Boundary Commission for the year* 1947, p. 6.) The various memoranda on local government reform published by the parties concerned also lend colour to this incessant conflict.

Councils.   Size again would depend on what is expected, and the relative abilities of these villages.

Finally, we would like to say this.   English experience has abundantly shown that it would be always wise to include in any local government ordinance a 'saving clause' allowing for periodic revision of local government boundaries no less than their functions.   This will enable young local government bodies to be started with light responsibilities which may be increased as they grow in experience and strength.

CHAPTER IV

FUNCTIONS, POWERS AND
RESPONSIBILITIES

OPINION is divided on the question of functions and
responsibilities which should be allowed to local
government bodies. In England, whither eyes from many
parts of the world are often turned for guidance and inspiration in matters connected with democratic institutions and
practices, recent years have seen radical redistribution of
functions formerly exercised by local government bodies.
This redistribution has resulted in substantial loss of powers
and responsibilities by minor authorities to major ones.
District Councils for instance have lost their functions and
powers in respect of elementary education (formerly their
sole responsibility), police, fire brigades, maternity and
child welfare, town planning and so on to County Councils;
while hospitals, electricity and gas, originally local government functions, have been nationalized; administration of
public assistance has gone to statutory Boards; and important roads have been taken over by the Ministry concerned,
with local government bodies acting as administering agents
only.

All these changes have led to much criticism particularly
among those who feel that too little discretion is now allowed
to local government bodies at any level, and too few responsibilities—many of them not important or interesting enough
to make it worth the while of talented would-be councillors
—are left, for instance, to smaller authorities of the county
district level. The fact remains that these changes were
really inevitable in the face of problems of cost, modern
technological advances, need for economy, efficiency and
uniformity. A well reasoned if heated argument has
recently been heard from an expert who felt that some of

the services, elementary education for instance, now transferred to the County Councils, could be more efficiently,
and perhaps more economically, run at lower levels. It
is quite acceptable that there are some services which could
be better run by an authority on the spot and closer to the
people; but there are others at the same time which occupy
the other extreme. The real problem has been, and will
remain for some time yet, where, if at all, the line should be
drawn; and whether it would be wise or even desirable for
a body like the State, which may be responsible for the
financial burden necessary for a whole service, to split
responsibility for the management of such a service between
different authorities, with whom it would have to deal
separately and individually, at different stages.

These points have been brought out here because they
are instructive to younger countries now evolving their own
systems of local government. These problems have not yet
been solved in England, and there appear to be a lot of
obstacles in the way of any swift solution. These obstacles
are not difficult to find, for they have all arisen from the hard
fact that, as far as local government is concerned, size,
functions and finance of the councils must be allowed free
interaction and settled *together*. In doing this, too, a long-
term view must be taken. This unfortunately was not
done early enough in England as is well evident from the
anomalies pointed out in the preceding chapter. That is a
mistake that every new country must take steps to avoid—
and that as early as possible, most advisedly at the very
beginning.

Once the size of the Council has been settled, the responsibilities or functions of such a council should to a great extent
be based on its financial, human and technical *ability* to
meet such responsibilities. These considerations would,
of course, mainly affect the question of efficiency. But, in
the new territories, tied to this question, there is also the one
of political training, which cannot be achieved without some
sacrifice, or readiness to accept lower standards of efficiency.

It follows, therefore, that in some aspects *ability* may have to be subjected to the need for political training and experience, and in others the other way round. The difficulty will always be where to strike the proper balance. In those territories where real political responsibility has been given to the indigenous people this decision will largely depend on the politicians; and how far such decision may be right or wrong will depend in turn on the experience and foresight of the politician concerned, how much he has got or is prepared to make use of expert advice, and how far he is able or prepared to modify his political doctrines or election promises in the face of realities.

Let us try to think of some guiding principle which may be useful in determining the functions of local government bodies without destroying or seriously weakening either or both of the two principal aims of local government in colonial territories. Services normally or conventionally performed or administered by local government bodies may be divided into three different categories:

(*a*) Those services, like education and medical care, requiring minimum standards the lowering of which would be to the national disadvantage, and the cost of providing which efficiently would definitely be quite beyond the capacity of an average local authority.

(*b*) Those services which, though not falling exactly into the previous group, are judged to be highly essential for the well-being of the inhabitants of a particular area, e.g. health and public sanitation. (The needs for this category of services may vary from area to area and may even be peculiar to a particular area or areas.)

(*c*) Other services which although essential or capable of adding to the general comfort and well-being of the people do not necessarily fall within the other two categories, e.g. markets, libraries, parks, etc.

In the first category of services the State cannot afford to stand aloof and leave it all to Local Authorities to manage the best they can. It must be directly concerned with the provision of the services and must be prepared to bear full or substantially greater financial and supervisory responsibility, even where the actual management or administration of the services may be entrusted to Local Authorities.   In the second category *ability* of the Local Authorities in all the aspects already mentioned might play a determining part. Where this is lacking the State should see to it that the services are not thereby automatically denied the people— and this may mean the State assuming, even if temporarily, some responsibility.   Where the ability is there, but the spirit is lacking in the authority concerned, it should be the State's place to compel their provision as a duty of the authority.[1]   In the last category such services will provide the necessary apparatus for political training, which is to remain an important aspect of local government development.   If this political training is to be healthily achieved, Local Authorities must be allowed full freedom and discretion, which may mean freedom and discretion to make mistakes, in the provision of the services.

All we have been trying to say here is that, as far as it is *reasonable and nationally safe*, or does not result in the neglect of important duties by them, Local Authorities should be allowed to get those services which they individually *deserve*, through their willingness and ability to meet the cost and bear other necessary responsibilities. That is the surest way of acquiring the necessary political training and responsibility.   It would then be left entirely to them to decide on what they want to have and proceed to raise funds to meet such needs and desires, or stop from taxing their people and doing without those services.   This means that as much as possible should be left to the individual initiative and enterprise of the local government bodies.   This automatically leads up to the question of specifying functions and powers in the Local Government

[1] The history of English Local Government shows that one of the early reasons for the State making financial grants to Local Authorities was in order to induce them to provide essential services which they otherwise would not have undertaken.

Ordinances which are to govern the local government bodies.

It is needless to say that any Local Government Ordinance laying down functions and powers for local government bodies should be simply drafted so as to be within reasonable understanding of the less educated members of the councils, free of ambiguity and, above all, make most of the functions *permissive* rather than *mandatory*—there should be more 'mays' and less 'shalls'; the latter should be confined to those subjects which it is in the interest of the authorities and of the public that the Local Authorities *must* have, e.g. adequate staff, health services, etc. This is the surest way of ensuring a healthy balance between the needs for efficiency and those for training and experiments.

An approach to this problem of allocation of functions to local government bodies will obviously be different in new and largely agricultural countries, from that which can be expected in an old and highly industrialized country like England; and even within these two classes of countries there will necessarily be essential differences between the various sections. That is why it was emphasized in an earlier chapter that any useful approach in any country should be based on the key questions: 'What are our special or peculiar circumstances, and where can we go from here?' Attempts were made there to show that hardly anything can grow from nothing: historical and environmental—which expression is taken to include social, economic and political —circumstances must all play joint and interactive roles in the growth and development of local government systems in different places and countries.

The Eastern Region of Nigeria is perhaps the first colonial territory in Africa where a wholesale experiment in the English practice was started in 1950. That part of the country was thought to be so lacking in tradition and strong political background as to provide a perfectly fertile and open ground for experimenting upon the 'English system-on-export'. Nothing need be added to what has already been said in previous chapters as to the satisfactoriness of this step. The Eastern Nigeria Local Government Ordinance of 1950[1] was, however, an embodiment of foresightedness for its elasticity, particularly as regards stipulation of functions and powers for local government bodies. The excellence of that Ordinance lay chiefly in the fact that the majority of the functions mentioned in it were *permissive* rather than *mandatory*—a fact which local authorities sometimes appear to lose sight of. The Ordinance as such did not specify functions for the various types of authorities, although it gave a long list of what they might do. It left specification of functions to be shown in the Instruments establishing the authorities; in other words, it was left for the Regional Authority or the Minister of Local Government to determine these in respect of individual Local Authorities. The wisdom of such a policy can hardly be over-praised, for it means assigning functions to local government bodies each according to *ability* or even need. This properly done would make local government a living day to day reality to the local communities.

In Appendix B to this book will be found relevant extracts from the sections of the old Eastern Nigeria Local Government Ordinance dealing with functions. (It has already been previously stated that, for convenience' sake, discussion in this book will, where necessary, be chiefly illustrated with material from that part of Nigeria supplemented by a study of systems elsewhere. To illustrate, therefore, our conception of how local government functions might be determined, it will be easiest for us to concentrate upon the functions contained in the Ordinance just mentioned.)

Local government should exist for the people and not the people for local government. The principal aim then of local government should be *community development*. This term is used here in a rather wide sense including not only the making of localities which are attractive and worth living in, by the provision of such things as good roads and

[1] It is being replaced by a new one.

so on, but also including the development of the different individual persons living within them, educationally, politically, and, if you like, socially and economically. And this clearly takes within its warm ambit our two pillar aims of local government—provision of social services and political training.

Bearing in mind the three types of authorities suggested in the preceding chapter, let us see how functions and powers might be distributed among them, beginning with the lowest authority.

(i) The Village Council

Generally speaking, the Village Council, or a council in that category which may be given quite a different name, is given too little responsibility to make membership on it attractive to many people, except perhaps in so far—as is the case in Nigeria—as such membership gives them an opportunity of being eligible for election to higher and more interesting Councils, the District and the County. Very often no specific functions are indicated for Village Councils either in the Ordinance or in the Instruments establishing them, with the result that the councillors, floating as it were on a wide sea of indefiniteness, are often ignorantly tempted to try the impossible, or at best the inadvisable. There were instances in Nigeria when Village Councils (sometimes known as Local Councils) passed resolutions to raise precepts for free primary education for the children of their area! There were other cases where councils honestly thought that the duty imposed on all councils to maintain law and order, as well as help to preserve peace, carried with it the right on the part of Village Councils to exercise judicial functions whereby they could try and punish the offenders.

Let us look at the following pertinent extracts from the Ordinance and an Instrument establishing a certain Village (*Local* in the Instrument) Council:[1]

[1] This Ordinance, as has been pointed out, is under active process of amendment and these extracts are taken from the old Ordinance for illustrative purposes only.

Section 85 (i) of the Ordinance reads as follows:

> It shall be the duty of *every council* established under this Ordinance to discharge the functions conferred by this or any other written law and generally to maintain order and good government within the area of its authority; and for this purpose, a council, *within such limits as may be prescribed by the Instrument* by which it is established, may either by its own officers, by duly appointed agents do all such things as are necessary or desirable for the discharge of its functions and for the maintenance of the health, safety and well-being of all persons living within the area of its authority. (Italics ours.)

Then turning to the Instruments establishing local councils in one of the areas one found the following:

> No specific functions are allocated to the Local Councils other than the powers conferred upon them specifically by the Ordinance or any written law; but the council may raise money by precept for and spend money on any project which is within the powers of *local government councils* as set out in the Ordinance or any other written law and which is approved by the Resident in charge of . . . Province as being of a *communal nature*. (Italics ours.)

Reading the above quoted section of the Ordinance without the Instruments one would interpret it to mean that since a Local (i.e. Village) Council came within the term 'every council' it would be within its powers under the Ordinance to build hospitals, secondary schools, maintain roads, etc., which were later shown in the Ordinance as functions which a local government body might undertake. Reading it with the Instruments establishing the particular Local Councils in question one was apt to ask what sort of projects were 'of communal nature' and what were not. The Instruments establishing cognate District and County Councils of the area in question clearly defined the functions of these Councils; could it then be that the intention was to allow 'residual' powers to Local Councils?

Far from trying to be unduly critical of the Ordinance in question, we have brought out the above points to show

how extremely necessary it is that Village (or Local) Councils should be clearly told in the Instruments, if not in the Ordinance, what functions should, or should not, be undertaken by them. It is true that, since any project to be undertaken by the Village or Local Council must first be approved by the Resident, nothing unreasonable will be allowed. That is perhaps all right for the present, but let it not be forgotten that the future of these officials is yet not quite settled in view of political developments. (See Appendix A.) What sort of functions then might be appropriately allowed to Village Councils?

For this class of local government bodies, an overall emphasis should be placed on 'Community Development' (which in this context must be more limited in scope than what we have previously seen). This should include such aspects as the provision and maintenance of markets; community centres (town or village halls); opening of village roads; postal agencies*; building of maternity homes*; provision and control of playing fields; building of primary schools*; control of animals, and so on.

All these matters, in varying degrees, are very dear to the heart of the average man in the village who regards most of them at least as of greater importance, from his own point of view, than any far-fetched matter. They are matters which directly affect him and his daily life, and it is on such matters that local initiative and responsibility as well as interest in local government as a whole must be built and developed.

Certain items above have been marked with an asterisk. Those are subjects which might require concurrent action or interest from higher or other authorities, such as the District Council or even a Voluntary Agency in case of school buildings. Roads opened or maternity homes built may ultimately have to be maintained wholly or partly by a higher authority, with whom prior consultation may be necessary.

The need for public playing fields and village halls is at present not generally well appreciated by many villages. It would certainly be of the utmost value to the villagers that places should exist where people, children as well as grown-ups, can, whenever they feel like doing so, resort for recreation or games, meetings or discussion, irrespective of their social standing or religion or other personal connections. If people appear now to be uninterested in such facilities, it is only because they do not see enough of them. The coming together in the way just described would go a long way to promoting real community feeling and intercourse so necessary in these days of mutual distrust and suspicion. Without going into any undue details, it might be mentioned that any community hall built should be adapted to the general needs and inclination of the people of the particular community concerned. Thus where people like dances, concerts and other cultural activities the hall should be adapted to these needs. Where people like to drink together provision might be made for this too! Local government would be 'stultified unless it is directed to the making of living communities and . . . deal with a wide range of things that people can use in common and can weave together into the texture of the sort of living they value.' (Cole: *Local and Regional Government*, p. 45.)

The control of animals is an age-long practice of village councils in African societies where farm crops are directly affected by the degree of control exercised over animals. This control might be regularized through the Village Councils and made to conform with requirements of civilized standards. Other functions of Village Councils would depend on the nature and aims of local government as a whole. Maintenance of law and order is, of course, an obligation no less on Village Councils than on other governmental institutions of a country. There may also be functions delegated to Village Councils by higher authorities, of which more later.

(ii) District Councils

With the exception of those functions which the Central Government may through the Instruments assign, or the

73

District Councils by agreement and wisdom voluntarily allow, to the Co-ordinating Authorities (and those functions which it may be considered best to allow to Village Councils) most local government functions should be performed at the District Council level. In addition to their legal and statutory functions, they may have also to perform a lot of delegated functions on behalf of the Central Government, particularly in those areas or territories which may wisely or unwisely decide to abolish the present offices of Administrative Officers or, what would amount to the same thing, where the present offices of Administrative Officers may decide to abolish themselves for lack of the right type of people willing to serve in them.

(iii) Co-ordinating Agencies or Councils

In a book entitled *Local and Regional Government*, Professor G. D. H. Cole has described and advocated what he calls Regional (and Joint Regional) Planning Authorities. For the benefit of those who have read that great work and who are likely thereby to get mixed up with our own Co-ordinating Agencies, we would like to point out categorically that the two kinds of authority have very little in common, although superficially they may appear to have resemblances. One or two fundamental differences between the two kinds of authorities might here be pointed out for the sake of clarification. That would also help to explain further our own conceptions of Co-ordinating Authorities which we tried to show in the last chapter.

Says Professor Cole: ‘I want it (i.e. the Regional Planning Authority) to be concerned fully as much with economic planning as with town and country planning in the narrower sense —that is to say, I want it to cover the local distribution of industries and services within the Region, subject to the general conditions determined by the national economic plan.’

We have no such conceptions at all for our Co-ordinating Authorities. Professor Cole no doubt was writing with a strong political bias which, of course, we do not have. Without in any way trying to enter into a controversy, particularly with that eminent authority, we would observe from the above quotation that its author seems to have in mind a country in which all industries are owned by the State, and in which local government bodies play their due part in the national economic or industrial machinery. We are not sure whether it would be accurate or fair to assume such a state in many parts of Africa—although nobody can be emphatically prophetic about the political or social future of any country.

Another thing Professor Cole has conceived about his Regional Planning Authority is that its members should be directly and popularly elected in the ordinary way. We do not necessarily advocate this for our Co-ordinating Authorities. (See Chapter IX.)

Speaking generally, we feel that Regional Planning Authorities having the size *and* the powers advocated for them in the book *Local and Regional Government, and* being constituted by direct popular election could easily be nothing less than small states within the country (as known in some countries) and cease to be local government bodies in the present conception of the term. Of lesser force is the other undesirable fact of having too many, and easily confusing, elections in the country, taking into account the already existing three or four different kinds of elections; and with due respect one might say that the solution suggested in the book in question does not appear to be very convincing from a practical point of view.[1]

[1] Professor W. A. Robson also favours for Local Government in England the establishment of regional councils, capable of recovering if possible the old local government functions—hospitals, public assistance, etc.—which have inevitably had to be transferred to *ad hoc* regional authorities of the Central Government chiefly because the existing organization, which is nearly 70 years old, has glaringly proved not only unsuitable but also incapable to meet the modern needs and requirements of these services. (See W. A. Robson: *The Development of Local Government* (third edition), pp. 59–68.)
The present writer has not as yet made careful comparison between Professor Robson's plans and those of Professor Cole to see where they agree or disagree. But, speaking superficially, Professor Robson's conception of the status, functions and place of *regional councils* would appear to have more appeal to us than Professor Cole's *regional authorities.*

75

We apologize for our 'presumptuousness' in taking the above points from that expert book so much to task. But we have been compelled into making the above remarks by a natural desire to clarify our position—which should not strictly be called criticisms. It is hoped, however, that the remarks have helped to explain the points we are driving at. As we shall see more of these proposed new bodies, the Co-ordinating Authorities, it should suffice here just to enumerate the sort of functions we consider might be assigned or allowed to them.

As was seen earlier, it would be most sensible, economical and efficient for more than one local government body to share in the provision or administration of certain services. Bearing in mind the services mentioned in the old Eastern Nigeria Local Government Ordinance (Appendix B) we would most tentatively suggest functions like the following for the Co-ordinating Agencies:

1. Education.[1]
2. Medical Services[2] (as opposed to Health Services which should be the responsibility of District Councils).
3. Town and Country Planning.
4. Afforestation and Forest Reserves.
5. Important Roads.
6. Newspapers and publications (Information Services).
7. Native or Customary Courts.
8. Water Supply.
9. Veterinary Services.
10. Negotiation for loans on behalf of District Councils.
11. Provision and maintenance of specialist and expensive staff whose services would be available to lower councils within the area of jurisdiction of the Co-ordinating Authority.

The above are mainly illustrative of the sort of services we feel might come within the responsibility of our Co-

[1] See page 78.
[2] See page 78.

ordinating Agencies. They are not intended to be 'hard and fast', nor can they be said to be anything near exhaustive. Local circumstances will, as usual, have the last word in each case.

Concurrent and Overlapping Services

It would be difficult—indeed unwise—to attempt to draw lines between functions that should be undertaken by, or powers that should be given to, the different tiers of local government bodies. There must certainly be an overlapping in many cases, and there may surely be services which it might be considered advisable or desirable to be undertaken concurrently by the different tiers; or even services which might financially be the responsibility of a higher authority but which it would be best to administer at a lower level. (Delegations of functions from a higher local government body to a lower one or from the Central Government to Local Authorities are many in England.)

All this leads to the conclusion that the old principle or doctrine (which has already broken or is breaking down even where it was born and fostered) that the different tiers of authorities could be independent of one another must now desirably, if not necessarily, give way to one of co-operation between the different tiers for the general good of all. This does not, of course, mean a position in which one authority should be regarded as necessarily *subordinate* to the other, but one in which one authority should look upon the other as a senior or junior partner in the 'business' of local government.

General

It must be realized that on the whole the resources of an average local government area in Africa are extremely poor indeed. The people are themselves very often in a state of abject poverty and cannot, therefore, contribute much to the revenue of the local authorities. With the possible exception of the few townships, there are hardly any forms of property upon which rates can be based. It follows,

77

therefore, that one of the main concerns (in some cases it might well be *the* main concern) of local government bodies could be to help in raising the economic standards of the people. Remember our statement above that *community development* should include *economic* development. This could be done in various ways. The simplest of these is perhaps the granting of scholarships to selected people to acquire technical or scientific skills, with a view to their coming back to their respective communities and translating their knowledge into practice for others to copy. It might not even be a bad idea for local government bodies to make advances or grant loans to such people on return from training for the establishment of their trades—agriculture or any other. Another method would be for the local authorities themselves to engage in such 'trading' or agricultural activities as would clearly provide a good lead and incentive for the people to follow. Such schemes should not be expected to yield short-term profits. They are most likely to be run at initial financial losses, but their long-term benefits would more than cancel out the initial losses.

Education and Medical Services

These two services were marked with numerals when included among the functions of Co-ordinating Authorities. They are services which are not only very expensive but nationally of the utmost importance. They are services which cannot conveniently and efficiently be financed by a local authority of any status and indeed wealth—without such authority abandoning or seriously neglecting other essential services. In Great Britain these services, once the full responsibilities of local government bodies, have now almost completely become the responsibilities of the State, which has either taken them over or assumed financial responsibility for their provision with local government bodies acting chiefly as administering authorities. (Hospitals are, in fact, managed by national Public or Statutory Boards.)

These are the two important social services whose urgency, benefits and needs the people most fully understand. In Nigeria the desire to supply them has been the foundation stone of many tribal and social unions and organizations. Some Village Councils have in the recent past passed resolutions to provide 'free' primary education for children living in their areas! This is, of course, fantastic, but it does show how keenly interested in education is even a Village Council. Tribal, clan and family unions have set up secondary schools and sent people to universities for training as educationists. Yet, quite paradoxically, there have been riots and disturbances in recent months over the payment of education rates demanded by local government bodies. There were many underlying causes for this unfortunate state of affairs, but perhaps the most fundamental was the people's *physical inability* to pay the education rates in addition to tax and other rates. Modern educational requirements and costs are such that to leave education in the hands of local authorities may well mean its ruin.

Turning to medical services the above arguments will apply *mutatis mutandis* with equal force. Hospitals should be the full responsibility of the Central Government, and might desirably be supplemented with cottage hospitals, dispensaries, maternity homes and *health* services provided by local government bodies.

The State as a whole has, and must admit, ultimate responsibility for the welfare of the people. Local government is but a device of convenience, and should not be understood to be alternative or substitute for State action or responsibility. It follows, therefore, that for the development and protection of its citizens, physically and mentally, the State should be responsible for the provision of such crucially essential services as Education and Medical Services. Where there are Voluntary Agencies and local authorities willing and able to undertake educational and medical work (as very often happens) they could be allowed

79

to do so with adequate financial aid and supervision from the Central Government. The question of compulsory education for children should not be simply approved in principle by a Central Government which then leaves it to the discretion of local government bodies to operate at their convenience, as indeed can possibly be the case. This may be a necessarily or even advantageously cautious move by a Government but it is bound to have quite undesirable and unbeneficial ultimate results. If and when the State feels it *can* provide compulsory education it should do so nationally rather than leave it to local authorities to attempt.

Central Government and 'Local Government' Services

It is then quite impossible to say with any degree of confidence and assurance where a line dividing the functions of local government bodies from those of the Central Government can be drawn. The inalienable fact, which we have already mentioned, is that in any country the ultimate and vicarious responsibility for the general welfare of the people rests with the National Government. It is a responsibility that cannot be shirked or even overlooked. That is the logic of all powers of local government bodies being derived from the National Government, which is morally bound to be interested in how local authorities do their job. Another thing which any responsible National Government should never lose sight of is the fact that a weak, inefficient or ineffective local government system is bound adversely to affect or reflect upon the National Government. If local government bodies must look upon themselves, as has been suggested, as important partners in the 'business' of government, the State must regard itself as the mother of these local government bodies, and must see that the children are well brought up and are doing well. This does not mean that the State should be an indulgent mother. As a wise and sensible parent her aim should be to nurse the children in such a way that they grow up strong and responsible, able to stand on their own feet in due course, and capable as time goes on of relieving their mother of some burdens and responsibilities.

It is clear, however, that until the relative wealth of the inhabitants of the various local government areas is substantially and visibly increased, thus making them better able to afford higher contributions into the funds of their local authorities by way of taxes and rates, the Central Government will continue to bear substantial burdens in the provision of essential services administered or executed by local government bodies. And this leads us to the question of finance.[1]

[1] See footnote at the end of Chapter V.

CHAPTER V

LOCAL GOVERNMENT FINANCE

'IT is a feature of Colonial finance only too familiar to
those who have some responsibility in that sphere that,
whereas in highly developed countries policy can be considered first and ways and means found thereafter, in the
Colonies generally speaking, policy must be adapted to the
available means which, by nature of things and for obvious
reasons, are elastic only to a very limited extent. This is
true, but painfully true of Native Administration (now
Local Government) Finance in Nigeria.' (Sir Sidney
Phillipson: *Financial Relations between the Government of Nigeria
and Native Administrations.*)

We could hardly find better remarks than the above with
which to open this crucial chapter. The above passage
truly emphasizes the relative poverty of local government
finance, and is a very good amplification of the points
which we attempted to bring out in the closing sections
of the last chapter. It shows the peculiar and rather unfavourable circumstances (financially) under which our
new local government bodies must work. Indeed, with the
complexity, diversity and great expensiveness of modern
needs, local authorities anywhere in the world cannot rely
solely or even mainly on their *local* resources to meet their
responsibilities. They must depend on external sources, on
the State and the Loan Market or Board, for a decisive
portion of the funds they need for carrying out expensive
services and capital projects. This is true of highly developed and wealthy countries, and will be much more
forcefully so of the less developed and much poorer
territories.

In Nigeria under the Native Administration system, and
until as late as 1947 or so, 'no logical distinction appears to

have been drawn between the objects of expenditure appropriate respectively to the government and the Native Administrations. The aim was to get useful things done, and the source of finance was a secondary matter.' (Sir Sidney Phillipson's Report.) Thus in some wealthy Native Administration areas, Native Administration funds could easily be used to finance projects, such as the building of trunk roads, which should properly be the responsibility of the Central Government. In the poorer areas Central Government funds could be used if available, for those things which should properly be a local responsibility. Of course, then there was only one principal source of revenue, the general tax, which was technically Government tax and belonged to the general revenue, with a fraction given to the collecting Native Authorities for their local needs. And even here there was much anomaly in the method of determining the shares between the Central Government and the Native Authorities. The shares were loosely based on the principle of need, with the result that the wealthiest and highly developed authorities very often paid proportionately smaller fractions of the tax they collected into the national revenue than the least developed and poorest Native Authorities. There were at the same time certain authorities whose income was so low that they paid very negligible (indeed virtually token) fractions, if any, of the tax they collected into the general revenue.

It was to regularize this confusing and anomalous state of affairs that Sir Sidney Phillipson was commissioned in 1946 to go into the whole question of financial relationship and responsibilities between the Central Government of Nigeria and the Native Authorities and since the publication of his report the position has become less unsatisfactory and uncertain. It is perhaps right to say that this unsystematic relationship between the Central Government and the Native Authorities was common to most, if not all, areas practising the Indirect Rule system.

With the advent of the new local government bodies a

situation more regular, more easily ascertainable and more systematic is, of course, necessary; and we shall now examine the different sources of revenue open to a modern local government body for the financing of its schemes and projects. The following nine items, arranged in their order of relative importance to the new Local Authorities, will be considered.

(a) Central Government Grants.
(b) Direct Taxes.
(c) Rates and Government Contributions in lieu.
(d) Loans.
(e) Licences.
(f) Earnings from Public Property and Commercial Undertakings.
(g) Fees.
(h) Fines and Penalties.
(i) Miscellaneous.

(a) Central Government Grants

By far the most important and most effective source of revenue for local government bodies must be Central Government Grants. The need and inevitability of this should already have been made clear in the preceding sections and chapters. In England, which is the most highly developed country in the world, the greater fraction of the money spent by local authorities in the provision of local services comes from the Central Government. In one County more than 60 per cent. of the County's revenue in 1953–54 came by way of Government Grants, and this did not include money given to the County by the Central Government for such things as the provision of houses under the Government's housing programme. It was also estimated that for the whole country the average of Government Grants to Local Authorities was 54 per cent.; and there is no reason to expect that these figures will not increase with the years. (It will be remembered that in

84

addition to these big grants the Government has already taken out of the hands of local authorities services like hospitals, roads, public assistance formerly the responsibility of local authorities.) The Grants are of two principal kinds—Percentage, etc., Grants and Equalization Grants. The latter as the name implies are aimed at at least minimizing the inequalities in resources existing between the different authorities (though it is almost impossible to remove the inequalities totally). They are based on a certain national average which, of course, excludes the wealthiest authorities from receiving them. The former on the other hand are paid to all authorities and cover a variety of items ranging from education and health services to rodent control (i.e. prevention of damage by pests!) If this happens in England how much more should it do so in the much younger, much poorer and much less developed territories of Africa?

(b) Direct Taxes

The differentiation between *tax* and *rate* may be said to be purely academic and one that may cause confusion. In a place like England the difference lies in the fact that *taxes* are collected by and paid to the National Government while *rates* (which are taxes on property) are collected by and paid to Local Authorities. In Nigeria the practice is *generally* the same as in England, but there are certain peculiarities. There is in Nigeria[1] the queer differentiation between Income Tax and what is called Schedule Two Tax, even though the two kinds of tax are taxes on income. They are called by different names according to who pays the tax, where it is paid, and to whom it is paid. Taxes paid by non-Nigerians all over the country, Nigerians resident in Lagos, and commercial firms, are classified as 'Income Tax' and belong entirely to the Central Government. Other taxes based on incomes and paid by Nigerians

[1] True at the time these lines were written.

85

in all places outside Lagos to their respective Native Administration or Local Government Treasuries are classified as Schedule Two Tax. There is also what is known as Schedule One Tax which is a sort of *poll* tax paid by those with very low or without ascertainable incomes. The Schedule One and Two Taxes are technically Government taxes, collected by or on behalf of the National Government, but almost the whole of what is collected is usually given back to the Local Authority (generally the Native Authority or District Council) of the area whence the taxes were derived. In most places of the Eastern Region of Nigeria, the National Government only retains sixpence per head of tax payers, while leaving all the rest of the taxes at source to the Native Administration, or District Council. Even those amounts retained by Government as *capitation taxes* (the 6d. per payer) are normally given back to the Local Authorities by way of what is known as Code Grants, but this time on the principle of *needs* rather than of *derivation*, with the result that in the end Government sends back practically *all* Schedule One and Two Taxes to the Local Authorities.

In point of principle there is room for improvement in the present system whereby the Local Authorities collect Government tax and keep the most substantial part of it themselves. The practice has gone on for so long that people—the Local Authorities themselves particularly— tend to lose sight of the fact that the tax is a Government tax at all, and this is often shown by their seeming failure to understand why the District Officers or the Resident (central government officials) should continue to exercise their powers under the Ordinance, especially where the new local government systems have been introduced. As further proof of this there was a case recently in which a District Council assumed powers conferred upon Administrative Officers under the Direct Taxation Ordinance!

There should be no argument that direct taxation is a Central Government concern, and its revenue a Central Government revenue. Local government bodies should be made to appreciate this fact as clearly as possible. One effective way of doing this would be for the whole of the revenue from Direct Taxation to be paid into Government Treasury or placed (for convenience' sake) on deposit in the Local Authority Treasuries, and from there the Government would pass over, formally each year, whatever it may want to give to the local authorities as a *general grant* to revenue of such Authorities. This point is important and the earlier it is given effective consideration the better it would be, otherwise serious complications might arise in the future. The present situation is but a legacy of one that was seen to obtain at the beginning of this chapter.

Revenue from this source could easily be increased, and one way of doing this would be by close and honest assessments of incomes. At present there are a lot of loopholes for fraudulent or sharp practices by the dishonest and the unscrupulous, and there are a lot of people, traders and private businessmen for instance, who are paying much less than their fair share. Another way would be the bold and right step of taxing women of ascertainable means. These would be women in regular employment and those carrying on private lucrative trade or business. The amount of revenue hitherto lost to public funds by the failure to do this is very considerable. Women are justifiably claiming equal rights with men. These they have almost completely got: they earn equal salaries with men, have now been given the franchise in some parts, and are entitled to representation by their own kind in the Legislative Houses of the country. But still they pay no taxes, not because they are unable to do so but merely because they are women. There could be no greater social injustice than that a woman drawing a salary of say £600 per annum, possibly from public funds, should contribute nothing to the general revenue by way of *direct* tax, while a man with perhaps only £30 per annum, or without any ascertainable income at all, pays tax. One is, of course, not advocating general taxation of women, for that would bring trouble from the illiterate and irresponsible sections; but there can be no justification for failing to tax women in salaried and regular employments as well as those in lucrative private business or trade. This class of women is responsible enough to realize that the present situation is nothing but an insult to their status and dignity, smacks of political immaturity for the nation, and cannot be a national credit in the eyes of the outside world. They must be given full rights of citizenship with men; yes, but let the rights be not only *full* but *fair*.

(c) Rates

As has already been remarked, rates are nothing but another kind of tax. They should, conventionally, be taxes on *property* rather than on persons or incomes. Unfortunately this is a rule that cannot be followed loyally in all areas (if in any at all) of African countries, particularly in the rural parts. In the rural areas of Eastern Nigeria, for instance, there are scarcely any properties, or hereditaments as they are often technically called, on which to base the rates, and so rates levied become nothing but additional 'tax' on persons and incomes. Under the old Eastern Region Local Government Ordinance a local government body could levy rates to perform practically any of its functions. In recent months the following kind of rates were introduced in many places in the Region by local government bodies: general rate, education rate, road rate, health rate, market rate, etc. In addition there were various 'precepts' made by Local (i.e. Village) Councils for the building of postal agencies, maternity homes, town halls, etc.

The above list is purely illustrative of what was happening, and to understand the position one has to refer to Section 99 of the old Eastern Region Local Government Ordinance to see the range of functions allowed to local government bodies and to think that for almost all the functions local government bodies might raise rates. A position such as this calls for restraint on the part of the rate-raising authorities who should keep their sense of proportion, and exercise plenty of caution in this question; otherwise the aggregate rates may easily and quickly turn out to be out of all proportion to the ability of the people to pay, and the result will be endless trouble, as evidenced by recent events. In one District the aggregate of rates and taxes paid by the local inhabitants suddenly rose by 200–300 per cent. of the tax (the only thing they previously paid) demanded from them the previous year—and this happened in the second year of the coming into force of the new Local Government Ordinance in that area.

Although the Local Government Ordinance appears to give the local government bodies 'blank cheques' in the matter of raising rates, it must be realized that the cheques if carelessly drawn can result in overdrafts and will be consequently dishonoured by the 'banks' concerned. The 'banks' in this context are, of course, the people who pay the rates.

The above situation will be worse in the Rural District Council areas than in the Urban Districts. Whereas in the former all (or most) rates are on persons and personal incomes—additional taxes in fact—in the latter there are usually many rateable hereditaments, and so rates can be *rates* in the conventional sense of the term. But this does not rule out the need for caution and restraint, which has been mentioned above, even in Urban District areas. (General remarks about rates are made, among other things, in the next chapter.)

The ever-necessary caution and foresight can only be forthcoming if the right type of councillors are available—a question discussed later in this book.

An important item which might be loosely included under this item is 'Government Contribution in lieu of Rates'. Technically, public buildings owned by the State Government in Local Authority areas are exempted from rates. But the State Government usually pays to such Local Authority a block sum as a contribution in lieu of rates.

This contribution could be described as 'grants' because it is the State Government and not the Local Authority which determines the amount payable, but it has fundamental differences from other grants.

(d) Loans

The average individual hates to be called a debtor, if he can help it. A public authority on the other hand may consider it desirable and expedient to be a debtor in order to carry out its functions and so may voluntarily decide to borrow. But like a private person it must be careful to borrow only to the extent that it is quite sure the amounts borrowed will be duly and conveniently repaid, for a public authority which cannot meet its loan liabilities would be just as dishonourable as, and perhaps even more dishonourable than, a private individual in similar circumstances.

Loans then constitute an important source of finance for a public authority. They make it possible to avoid excessive or unduly burdensome taxation, and constitute the most popular method of financing capital works. In England a Local Authority may contract loans even for the purpose of purchasing motor vehicles and pay it back with interest within a period of eight years. The period for the repayment of loans is often determined by the estimated life of the object for which the loan is raised. Thus a loan for building a house can be repaid over a period of sixty years. In many countries loans by local government bodies are usually made by the National Treasury or by any other source approved by the National Government, and amounts to be borrowed are also controlled by the National Government.

Since loans must naturally be refunded, it follows that, although they may alleviate or postpone it, they do not eliminate taxation. But they are defended on grounds of *convenience* and of *equity*. *Convenience*, because the people will not be suddenly called upon to pay excessive taxes and rates, but will be able to meet necessary and urgent expenditure by instalments, by refunding small portions of the loans with interest over a number of years. *Equity,* because the actual beneficiaries of the public undertaking may be members of a future generation more than of the present. An example of such an undertaking is afforestation or, in the case of a National Government, provision of railways, building of docks, etc.

Loans may not be incurred for the purpose of meeting recurrent expenditure such as staff salaries, etc.

(e) Earnings from Public Property and Commercial Undertakings

Under the old Eastern Region Local Government Ordinance local government bodies were empowered to engage in commercial undertakings; in other words, they might invest part of their revenue in projects that would earn profits and extra revenue over a number of years.

It is important that the new local government bodies should not lose sight of this item. A public authority which could raise say £1,000 as rents from public property such as houses and land, profits from sales of farm produce, incomes from services provided—such as water supply and electricity, etc.—would need to raise £1,000 less rates and taxes to meet its obligations.

Local authorities could own and run public transport as in fact is the case in many advanced countries. They could charge moderate fees for the use of stadia, town halls, etc. They could in short so manage it that even essential services provided bring in some money. Thus a Village Council which wanted to build a postal agency, could so plan it that one side of it was suitable for renting out as a shop or office to people having the need for such facilities; and in that way the building would serve not only the purposes for which it was intended but also be a revenue earning asset.

(f) Licences

A vigilant and careful local authority should be able to

profit much from this item of revenue. Bicycles, dogs, trading houses and a host of other things properly selected could be subject to licensing by local authorities.

(g) Fees

These are sums of money charged by a local government body for services rendered to private individuals. A few examples will do. Money paid into the County Council Treasury for services of a County Surveyor preparing plans for a land case which is before a Native Court comes under this head; also fees for registration of births and deaths, and so on. In short payment for services rendered by public officials, *which are not of a business nature*, are affected here. Granted favourable conditions, this can be a very helpful source of revenue.

(h) Fines and Penalties

These constitute another, though not so important, source of revenue for some local government bodies. They should be easily understood and will need no lengthy discussion. *Fines* will normally come from Native or Customary Courts. *Penalties* are paid when somebody offends against some regulation of a local authority. They may be paid in, or outside, the Court, and their amounts are normally well known in advance. An example is money paid by an owner of an animal caught and impounded by a local authority, before reclaiming such an animal.

Neither fines nor penalties should be regarded as a sure, stable or even honourable source of income. They are usually 'bad' money. The more citizens become law-abiding the less the incomes from this source will be, and it cannot be a good reflection on a society whose income under this head is always on the increase!

(i) Miscellaneous

Under this head will come odd moneys which cannot be

classified under any of the above heads—gifts and forfeitures for example.

Conclusion

Contrasting the position of our new local government bodies with that of the Old Native Authorities, one sees how the new bodies are in a much stronger position than the old authorities which they are now replacing. The present local government bodies have the powers to levy rates and powers to raise loans which the old Native Authorities scarcely had. The old Native Authorities were often restricted in the expenditure of their funds; a minimum yearly surplus was insisted upon, and the Native Authorities were generally required to invest their 'surplus' funds overseas. Under the modern system, judging from the English practice, restriction upon spending existing funds is most likely to be relaxed. Local government bodies raise moneys by way of rates for specific purposes and are expected to use up the rates for the purposes intended. Similarly grants are paid for specific purposes and must be used up for the purposes intended. In England it would be regarded as an 'offence' for a local authority to have an unreasonably large surplus, if any at all, at the end of the financial year; and should a surplus exist, it must be credited to the revenue for the following year with proportionate reduction in the amount of rates to be demanded. In the Eastern Region of Nigeria some sort of surplus is still required, and this, no doubt, is a relic of the past, as it is very often not advisable to break too suddenly with the past! It is also a prudent step. For it is desirable that local authorities should have something left from their incomes after meeting their obligations against unexpected expenditure, such as sudden and unforeseen increase in staff salaries, retiring benefits and—though we should not be regarded as wishing them ill—various compensation and court expenditure should they be compelled as a body corporate, to go to court.

93

Mention has been made of the old Native Authorities investing their surplus funds overseas. This was not a very popular course of action, particularly among those who did not fully understand the expediency or even necessity of it. It therefore met with much criticism. The reason for taking the course was that there were no safe and profitable opportunities for such investments in Nigeria. The overseas investments brought in a steady 5 per cent. interest and were 'gilt-edged'—the only kind of investment suitable for public money. It is not very likely that our new local government bodies will need to invest their money in this way, but should such a need arise, it is hoped that there will be opportunities for such investment locally.[1]

[1] Fifteen months after the drafting of this book but shortly before its publication the Government of the Eastern Region of Nigeria has taken another revolutionary step in its financial relationship with local government bodies. Readers will remember that this region was the first in Africa to experiment on the English system of local government. Appendix C summarises some provisions of the 1955 Local Government Ordinance (also passed after the draft of this book). In that Appendix we have expressed the view that the 1955 Ordinance is more realistic than the 1950 Ordinance which has now been repealed.

As the proofs of this book are being read, the Eastern House of Assembly (Parliament) has passed a Finance Law enabling the Government to take over the collection of all taxes hitherto collected by local government bodies, and limiting the amount of rates which a local authority may collect to five shillings, unless with the prior approval of the Minister. That Law also provides for the taxation of women in salaried employment in the whole region, whose incomes exceed £100 per annum, and also women traders in specified towns whose incomes also exceed £100. Henceforth, services hitherto undertaken by local government bodies would be largely financed with grants from the Central Government.

CHAPTER VI

GENERAL COMMENTARY INTERLUDE
ON LOCAL GOVERNMENT FINANCE

IN the preceding chapter the various ways by which a local authority can raise the money it needs for carrying out its functions or services were discussed. It would now be useful to pass some general comments on local government finance.

It has been seen that a local authority's own chief source of income in most African Colonial territories at the present time, and for some years to come, is taxation, which includes rates. In the rural areas, where no rateable forms of property exist, it was seen that rates are mainly personal and direct—indeed, nothing less than additional taxes. Everybody knows how unpopular a tax is to any person called upon to pay it, particularly when it is direct and personal. Unfortunately, a local authority has very limited, if not niggardly, productive forms of indirect taxation. The lucrative forms of indirect taxation, e.g. customs and excise duties, generally belong to the National Government of a country.

Rates in any country are not fair or equitable forms of taxation. They are usually *regressive* in incidence. That is to say, the burden falls more on the poor than on the rich. Take as an example rates on property. These are, more often than not, based on an assessed value of the hereditaments rather than on the income values of such hereditaments or even on the financial ability of the payer. As a matter of fact, where the property is, say, a house let out to tenants the rates are virtually indirect taxes on the poor tenants who pay them through increased rents. The unfairness of this is further pronounced by the fact that the poorer people with large families must live in bigger houses, and therefore pay more rent which includes rates, than richer ones with no families. It also happens that, where rents are not controlled by the State, any increase in rates by a public authority merely affords landlords and landladies a good pretext for putting up rents and making profits thereby.

This unfairness of the rating system, coupled with the desire to 'freeze', if not reduce, the present dependence of local authorities on assistance from the State by way of grants has led many people to consider various methods of increasing local government revenue. Three such methods proposed may be mentioned. They are: (1) Increased charges of fees discussed under (g) in the last chapter; (2) Basing rates on site values; (3) Raising a local income tax.

(1) *Increased Fees.* This might be possible, but it can certainly not bring much relief to local authorities. Besides there is the possible criticism that any undue increases in such charges would be unfair if not anti-social, and might in fact drive people into making use of private facilities, thereby making the local authorities lose even the little revenue they might previously have been having under this head. For the same reason, unreasonable raising of prices under the heading of earnings from public property or commercial undertakings discussed under (e) in the last chapter would be vigorously opposed. As a matter of fact there is a school of thought which is definitely opposed to public authorities engaging in any trading activities, such as the running of public transport or owning of public farms. Such people are prepared to support such activities by the State only if charges for them to the public are definitely lower than what private enterprises charge, thereby granting relief to the public at large who want to make use of the facilities. This might well mean public authorities running such business at a loss! Opposition can also be expected from

private enterprisers who cannot view with favour any attempt by a public authority to compete with them in their business.

(2) *Site Rates.* This might well be a good source of raising revenue, or at least counteracting some of the injustice of the rating system. But it can best be applied in towns rather than in rural areas. Since, however, under our suggested organization towns would be part of rural areas, the latter could indirectly benefit from such rates raised in the towns. This system of site rating has been successfully operated in South Africa, New Zealand and Australia. The system is defended on the ground that values of property are very often enhanced as a result of public funds being used in the improvement of the area, for instance by the opening of roads, improvement of layout, establishment of market sites, and so on.

(3) *Local Income Tax.* From our discussion of the position about rating in the rural areas of Eastern Nigeria, it will have been clear that a sort of local income tax already exists there, because of the absence of rateable property. In a certain area of that part of the world, 7d. in the £ is charged on all ascertainable incomes and those who have no ascertainable incomes pay a flat rate of 18s. 8d.; both of these in addition to the national tax. It would certainly be a fairer means of raising local revenue than rating. But it cannot be thought that it could replace *rating*; and if, but only if, it were possible to apply it successfully, it might only usefully supplement and reduce rates. Unfortunately, it would be administratively very difficult to operate such a tax. Proper assessment would be difficult if not impossible in many cases, and it might even dangerously undermine the national taxation policy. The example of Canada, where it was given a trial and abandoned, shows how difficult it is for a local authority to operate such a tax along side the State. It is also our contention, as should already be evident from what we have said in the previous chapter,

that taxes, in the present understanding of the term, should belong to the State which should have one common policy or principle for the whole country. There would be nothing to prevent the State from making any grants it wishes to the local authorities from the taxes, collected by or for it, afterwards. As a matter of fact, with increased responsibilities for the State which may be compelled to finance its development schemes through increased taxation, it is possible to see that the position such as described about Nigeria cannot long endure.

Mention was also made of loans in the last chapter. The powers of local authorities in this respect are very limited, and controlled in most countries by the State through legislation and other methods. Generally, local government loans must be raised internally in the country, by methods and from sources approved by the National Government. This is not an unwise policy, if the experience of a country like Germany is to provide a useful lesson. In Germany some municipalities became bankrupt after the First World War as a result of too liberal a policy in this respect by the National Government.

This question of State interference or control leads one back to the question of rating or taxation by local authorities. Local authorities are, of course, subordinate to the State, and their policies must be directly governed by the general policy of the State. Thus, if it is the State's policy to encourage industry, trade or agriculture and so on, it may decide to do this by granting tax reliefs to these industries. Such reliefs would not be effective if local authorities were to continue rating these industries highly. Thus in England there is what is known as 'derating', which means relieving the industry or trade, which it is intended to encourage or promote, partially or fully from paying rates. Agriculture and industry were in this way 'derated' in 1929, the former fully and the latter partially, the Central Government making grants to the local authorities affected in lieu of their loss of rating incomes from these sources. It is, however, at present strongly felt in many quarters that it is high time these items were 're-rated' since they are now doing well and hardly need any encouragement or protection.

CHAPTER VII

SUPERVISION AND CONTROL OVER LOCAL GOVERNMENT BODIES

IN this short chapter we wish to go into the rather vexed question of control and supervision of local authorities. We saw in the third chapter that the term 'Local *Self-Government*' was greatly misleading, for local government bodies *cannot* be *self-governing* in the real sense of the term. The reason is simply that they derive not only their powers but also in many cases the very substantial part of their funds from an external authority—the State. Naturally, if a greater body gives a lesser one powers and funds to administer, such a greater body would be reproachably careless or irresponsible if it did not ensure that the powers were properly exercised and not abused or even shelved, and also that the funds were well and economically used. To do this the greater body must want to know what the lesser body is doing and to express disapproval if something goes wrong. This is *supervision* and *control*, which many local authorities resent, and some critics condemn.

But what are the alternatives to this supervision and control? The first alternative would be for the State to cease to have anything to do with local government bodies. This might mean not retaining the right to grant them powers and/or not giving them any financial assistance. Clearly such an attitude would be disastrous. It would lead to national incoherence, indiscipline and confusion; it would lead to inefficiency, social suffering and injustice; it would lead to waste; and it would be a serious retrograde step, which no one certainly would wish to see.

The other alternative would be for the local government bodies to continue to derive their powers and the greater part of their funds from the State, but without the latter wishing to know what happens afterwards. This would be clearly impossible. The State Government owes a duty to all the citizens to see that their tax is not only spent in proper ways and most beneficially, but also to ensure that general welfare and social justice is as far as possible maintained. This rules out the argument mentioned earlier (Chapters III and VI) that local authorities could regain their 'independence' by finding local means of financing their projects—for instance, by raising the theoretical 'local income tax'.

The State then must continue to exercise its powers of supervision and control over local government bodies. But this control and supervision must not be confined to the State, which necessarily requires the co-operation and assistance not only of the general public but of the elected councillors themselves.

Naturally different methods of supervision and control are adopted by the State in different countries. In England the control and supervision takes three forms of which the first two mentioned below are of general applicability. They are: (1) Ministerial control exercised either by the Minister concerned or a Government Department on his behalf; (2) Judicial control; (3) Control of one authority over another.

(1) *Ministerial or Department Control.* This is done through the power to withhold grants unless certain conditions are fulfilled; the power to sanction loans which a local authority may want to contract; by means of audit and the power to surcharge the councillors for funds deemed to be improperly spent. In addition the Minister has powers to approve certain staff appointments; and Ministers are empowered to make regulations governing the conduct of local government bodies, which regulations have the force of law. There is also the right of any citizen to appeal to the Minister against the conduct of a local authority which may adversely affect him (this is known as *administrative appeal*) and the right of inspection and general supervision which a Minister

or a Department official has over local authorities. Lastly, there are the *default* powers, whereby a defaulting authority may be compelled to do its duty or defray the cost of such duty if done by another body or person, with powers for the Minister to suspend or cause the arrest of such local authorities as may fail to carry out these latter instructions.

(2) *Judicial Control.* Local authorities are legal creations, and so it follows that should it fail to act in conformity with its rights and powers within the law it should be answerable before a court of law. Let it be remembered also that as 'corporate' bodies local government bodies have the right to sue and be sued for debt, for breach of contract, for misconduct, for injury or damage to person or property and so on. But their special or peculiar nature makes it difficult, except by the Court, to know off-hand when it is liable and when not.

(3) *Control of one authority over another.* A County Council has powers to approve or sanction loans to be contracted by minor authorities, e.g. the Parish Council, under its jurisdiction. It also has powers to act in *default* and powers to alter boundaries of minor authorities. These powers are rather limited to certain authorities, and, unlike the first two, are not of general application.

All these show the methods adopted in England for the control of their local government bodies. In a later chapter we shall cast a glimpse at what happens in some other countries. In such places as the Eastern Region of Nigeria, where the new reforms have already taken place, the English methods are very largely followed. There are there the Judicial control and the power of audit, as is the case in England, but by far the most decisive control rests with the Regional Authority at the centre, which has very wide powers indeed. These powers are here summarized:[1]

---

[1] This was the position as existed under the 1950 Ordinance which is now being replaced, but it is safe to anticipate that the new Ordinance will not reduce these powers, which may in future have to be exercised by the Ministry.

(i) The Regional Authority has the powers to amend any Instruments establishing any local government council. Such an amendment may take the form of changing the name of the council, altering the status and/or constitution of the council, and modifying or altering in one way or another the functions of any council.

(ii) The Regional Authority has the power to alter the areas of authority of any council. Such alteration may take the form of adding to or subtracting from the areas, division or fusion of areas of councils, and so on.

(iii) The Regional Authority has the power of dissolving a council. Failure on three consecutive occasions to hold meetings with enough frequency as required by the Ordinance; failure to fulfil the requirements of the Ordinance for instance in the levying of rates; failure to apply a council's revenue properly; and failure to conform to statutory obligations, may all lead to the dissolution of a council.

(iv) 'If any council shall fail to do or carry out any work or thing . . . or should fail to make, revoke or enforce any bye-laws' as it is empowered to do, and such failure constitutes, in the opinion of the Regional Authority, 'a grave menace to health, safety or welfare of the public within or without the area' of such council the Regional Authority may by notice require the council to take the necessary measures, and if the council, without good cause, should still fail to do so, the Regional Authority may himself cause necessary bye-laws to be made in order to abate and remove the danger and may authorize any person or persons to undertake any works or duties that should have been undertaken by the council concerned.

The above are the most important, but by no means the only powers of the Regional Authority over local government bodies in Eastern Nigeria.

For instance, mention has not been made of such purely administrative, executive or routine functions of the Regional Authority as the approving, amending or otherwise of the estimates of the big councils—the County, the Urban District, and the Rural District Councils; the approval or otherwise of the appointment of senior members of the Local Government staff, or even his powers to enforce certain functions—apart from those mentioned in (iv) above—of a District Council which may be judged to have failed in its duty to carry out such functions properly.

How does the Regional Authority go about the exercise of his powers summarized above? And how does he know when it is necessary to exercise such powers? These are important questions—questions which the average man and woman in the street would like answered. Let us consider the last question first.

How does the Regional Authority know when it is necessary to exercise his powers? Perhaps the simplest answer is that events have wings with which they can easily fly to the ears of the Regional Authority. But more important than that, the Regional Authority depends on the general public and well-meaning councillors to tell him when and where things go wrong.

The State requires the co-operation and assistance of the public and honest councillors in the difficult but necessary task of supervising and controlling local government bodies. A vigilant public and courageous councillors made it possible for it to be known some time ago that all was not well in the old Lagos Town Council, and this led to the appointment of a Commission of Enquiry into the affairs of that Council which was later dissolved. There are recent cases in the Eastern Region also which Commissions of Enquiry have been appointed by the Minister of Local Government to probe into.

Everyone then has a duty to perform in this respect. If the public is too timid, too indifferent or too careless to play its full part, it will be failing in an important duty. There is something even further than that. If the public shows itself ready and capable of exposing the council's failures, it can in a great way help the councils themselves to survive;

for it will then make the councils sensitive about their positions and so carry out their duty in the best way possible. There is also the other side to the question. The public must not consider it its principal and only duty to look out for the failures of the councils to expose and condemn. It is equally the duty of the public to look out for the successes of the councils to acclaim and praise—to encourage and co-operate with the councils in the successful performance of their duties. In some ways, this second role of appreciation and encouragement on the part of the public may even be more important than the one of finding faults and condemning the councils. But the most important thing is that, whether we praise or condemn, we should be sure that our action is in the public interest— without malice, without bitterness and without prejudice.

Now to the first question, how the Regional Authority sets about the exercise of his powers. He does not and cannot act arbitrarily. The Ordinance provides that before he exercises any of the powers conferred upon him, proper and open enquiry or investigation must be conducted. He must appoint a suitable person or persons to conduct such enquiries. At and during such enquiries the council affected is given adequate opportunity of making representations and defending itself, its actions and its attitude. The proceedings at such enquiries may take the form of proceedings in a Court of Law, with opportunity to call and examine witnesses. Even where the Regional Authority 'may of his own motion and in his absolute discretion, on the application of any persons concerned, if he shall think fit, revoke the Instrument establishing any council, if he considers it in the interests of the persons living within the area to do so', the council concerned can still be given an opportunity of making representations in writing.

That is a fair arrangement, fair to the councils, to the public and to the Regional Authority himself. The councils concerned are thus able to defend themselves against any charges preferred against them; the general public is able to hear both sides and know exactly where the fault lies; and the Regional Authority is better able to be properly informed before making up his mind whether to exercise his powers or not. The provision for such public enquiries also acts as a check to mischief-makers who might merely delight in levelling unfounded charges against councils to cause confusion; for such mischief-makers would not find it to their advantage to make charges which they cannot substantiate.

Most readers will agree that there is a strong case for some of these powers to be decentralized.[1] There is nothing that can be lost by such decentralization; on the other hand there is a lot to be gained by it. It is interesting to note here that the Governments of the Western Region of Nigeria and of the Gold Coast, whose Local Government Ordinances largely follow the pattern set by that of the Eastern Region of Nigeria, but were drafted and passed later, have made provisions for desirable decentralization—the Western Region of Nigeria by the system of having Local Government Inspectors and wide delegation of powers to these officers on the spot, and the Gold Coast by the latter system of delegation of powers no doubt to Administrative (or other) Officers on the spot.

There can be no doubt that these are very sensible provisions in the light of the political circumstances of the areas or countries concerned, which are such that there can be no getting away from the fact that the Central Government through their own officials must participate more or less directly in the conduct of local government affairs. Other new countries would be well advised when forming their own Local Government Ordinances not to lose sight of this fact.

That cannot make the system cease to be local government as some people would suggest—it would simply be a child of the special circumstances of African administrative history. It would not even be peculiar, since examples of

---

[1] The new Eastern Region Local Government Bill has made provision for some decentralization.

such practice from other countries are many, as will be seen in our chapter on 'Other Systems'. The new local government bodies need proper guidance, which can best come from the central Government. The territories are poor in human resources—are lacking in people well qualified to discharge local government functions without the assistance of the Central Government which almost exclusively has a monopoly of well qualified officials.

In Chapter IX, Section (d) we have discussed what the new relationship between a Central Government official and the new local government bodies might be.

CHAPTER VIII

COMPOSITION AND CONSTITUTION
OF COUNCILS

ONE chief complaint against the old Native Administration system—the system of Indirect Rule—was that young men of talent and education scarcely had any place on its councils. The reason for this was, of course, inherent in the principle of 'Indirect Rule' itself which was government through 'indigenous authorities'—i.e. chiefs; and since younger people hardly attained that distinction, they were naturally barred from the Native Administration councils. As a result (see Chapter II) the more dynamic nationals saw in the system a tendency to favour, shelter and strengthen illiterate, conservative, unprogressive and sometimes even autocratic chiefs at the expense of the younger educated elements. But it would be both difficult and unfair on our part to agree here that the member-chiefs of the old Native Administration Councils generally deserved these uncomplimentary epithets. It would not be true for instance to say that all those who, by virtue of their social position, had been made members of the old Councils were uneducated and unprogressive, for there were often to be found among them really educated elements—men who either had retired from public or other 'literate' services before appointment to the Native Authority, or had succeeded to their fathers' positions quite young where chieftaincy was hereditary. As to the charge of conservatism we can only say that human nature is intrinsically conservative and that conservatism is not *per se* a bad thing—except where it becomes detrimentally obstructive. As to the charge of autocracy we can only say that we have not known much about that in recent times.

Membership of a Native Authority was not, however,

automatic upon one becoming a chief or traditional leader of one form or another. Appointment of Native Authorities was the sole prerogative of the Governor on the advice, of course, of Administrative Officers—his representatives—on the spot. It followed then that anybody judged to be out of favour with the Government had very slender chances of being appointed a Native Authority or member of a Native Administration Council. This was quite natural, for the Central Government had direct responsibilities in and for matters of local administration—which was but an element of central administration—and nobody would have expected the Governor to appoint to the Native Administration Councils people known to be against the Government or its policy, or judged to be otherwise incapable of holding the office—any more than one would expect a Prime Minister to appoint members of the Opposition or other political opponents to his Cabinet.

With all the best intentions in the world, the practice, such as it was, was, basically, bound to lead to some misunderstanding and unpopularity, particularly among those desiring to serve but having no opportunity. A chief approved for appointment by the Government was not always the most popular among his people. This, however, must not be carried too far, for it was a general principle defined by that chief apostle of Lugard, Sir Donald Cameron, that as far as possible chiefs acceptable to the people should be appointed. They were appointed on their personal merits and record. And the few who were perhaps appointed against the wishes of the masses (by no means deliberately) constituted enough ground upon which those interested could stand and condemn the 'unfairness and unrepresentativeness' of the whole system.

This attack was often enhanced by the unpraisewo1thy attitude of the Councillors themselves—which should perhaps not be very surprising. For, owing their position by appointment to the Administration, rather than to their people through election, these Councillors sometimes behaved as if they did not consider that the opinion of the people they served mattered at all in their daily conduct, so long as they did not offend the Authorities who gave them their office. Some of them even appeared to give the impression that they were the masters—perhaps this was not surprising in view of their social status as traditional leaders and rulers—rather than the servants of the people and, what was still more reproachable, scarcely took the trouble to tell their people what had been decided in the Councils or even what the Government had told them, in the sole belief that they *would* pass the information on to the people they represented. This failure on the part of the Councillors to keep their people adequately informed of what was happening frequently led to ignorant opposition by the latter to useful schemes of development as well as to a general distrust of the Councillors' intentions; particularly as there were always forces outside the Councils ready to exploit such situations.

Nevertheless, local government development, despite the above features, had been steadily progressing—laying valuable foundations for our modern systems, the constitution of which we must now discuss.

(a) Elected Councillors

Modern authorities are constituted mostly by election and not, as was the case with the old ones, by appointment. Everybody qualified under the Ordinance is eligible to be elected a councillor or to join in electing others. A most important advance which has generally been made is that all tax and rate payers, provided they are not disqualified in other ways, are eligible to vote or be voted for, which means that, even in those areas where there is as yet no universal adult suffrage, women of property who pay rates are not only able to join the men in electing councillors but also qualified to be elected councillors themselves.

The methods of election vary, of course, from place to

COMPOSITION AND CONSTITUTION OF COUNCILS

place. Generally speaking, the higher councils (the District and County Councils in Eastern Nigeria and their equivalents in Western Nigeria and the Gold Coast) are elected indirectly through electoral colleges which in most cases are simply the lower councils. In Eastern Nigeria, for instance, District Councils are elected through the Local (i.e. Village) Councils, whose duty it is also in certain cases to elect members from among their number to form the electoral colleges for the County Councils—where the Local Councils are not large enough to be authorized by the Instruments to elect members direct to the County. (The new bill is likely to alter this to the method of universal adult suffrage.)[1]

In the Gold Coast the Local and Urban Councils (which are equivalent of District Councils in Eastern Nigeria) are electoral colleges for the District Councils (the equivalent of County Councils in Eastern Nigeria). In urban areas, generally, where elections are done through wards they are fairly direct.

Under the old system Village Councils usually comprised all the male inhabitants of the Village concerned, normally summoned to meetings by beating of gongs, ringing of bells or other traditional methods of announcement. Under the modern systems only a few people, selected by election, constitute the Village Councils. We shall see later that one unfortunate result of this new practice has been the exclusion, in many cases, of really influential and important traditional dignitaries or authorities, to the serious discomfort, at times, of the constituted Village Councils.

In respect of election in the Rural Areas (speaking here mainly of Eastern Nigeria) the Resident in charge of the Province appoints returning officers, usually to conduct the elections. But in the Municipalities and Urban Districts

[1] The new Eastern Nigerian Local Government Law (No. 26 of 1955) provides that, except in special cases, Councils shall, as far as possible, be elected by means of universal adult suffrage.

an Administrative Officer is normally appointed to conduct only the *first* or *initial* elections, after which the Town Clerk or Urban District Secretary is permanently appointed by office to be the returning officer for subsequent elections. (No details yet about what the new bill proposes to do.)[1]

It is not the intention at this stage to criticize the methods of election as briefly described above. By themselves, they appear the most suitable in the present circumstances, and it might even prove disastrous to rush into changes before the people have fully adjusted themselves to the new conditions and get to know exactly what they are doing. The slight hitches which, in our judgment, are present here and there in the methods of constituting the councils, will become apparent as we proceed with the discussion in the succeeding sections of this chapter. For this section one or two general remarks will suffice.

A discerning observer of local government elections in the areas where the new systems have been introduced will be easily struck by two unpleasant characteristics—parochialism and corrupt practices of one form or another. The former, however, should not be unduly startling for areas where political responsibility is only just beginning to develop and where loyalties to a family or clan are still too strong to be subjected to wider national issues with which the majority of the people are only unintelligently familiar.

Although parochialism must be discouraged in every way possible, it is not necessarily a bad thing at this stage of local government development—so long as the methods used do not stultify other aims of local government, for sensible local loyalties could easily be harnessed into wider loyalties on a national scale; they may in fact be the only foundation upon which to build. On the other hand,

---

[1] The new law has removed all references to Resident; but it is most likely that, as Local Government Commissioner, this officer will continue to perform—even more directly than under the old ordinance of 1950—this and other functions on behalf of the Minister, whose powers may be delegated to him. See Appendix C.

corrupt practices, the principal of which is bribery, in matters connected with public business are radically evil, and, to say the least, absolutely incompatible with the useful aim of using local government as a basis of training for national political responsibility. No method employed to suppress it could be too strong, or too drastic.

Evils die very hard once they establish roots in society. Our local government must not be allowed to develop on a foundation of corruption, which is bound to undermine and may finally destroy the social and political fabric of a whole country. If strict and close, central control, at least in the initial stages, would help to check and finally destroy this evil of bribery, and that would not be too high a price to pay for the healthy development of democratic local government in young countries. The evil effects of gaining seats on local government councils through bribery and corruption are many and obvious, and without going into great details we would here like to mention a few of the most direct ones on the local government body or bodies affected.

First, bribery and corruption will keep out of the councils good men of integrity and ability who will not be willing, quite rightly, to bribe in order to serve. Secondly, they will confirm the belief, already existing among the less informed classes of the population, that councillors go to councils to share some booty—most probably their rates—rather than to serve them. Thirdly, the councils may in time become privileged places for corrupt men of no character. Fourthly, and perhaps most important, those who get into the councils by corrupt means cannot themselves be expected to be incorruptible.

None of the above bad effects need any gloss or elaboration. Services on local government councils are generally expected to be free, that is to say, councillors do not expect any financial gains or payments. What then does a person paying over £50 as bribe to electors expect to gain from his membership on the councils? Of course, he should expect nothing except the honour of being able to serve and work for the benefit of the people. But it would be foolish to conclude that the large bribes are paid merely in order to have an opportunity of serving the people. For the right explanation one needs only to notice the wrong and un-qualified staff appointments, prostitution of contracts, wrong assessments of taxes and rates, etc., which take place in some councils. Where these have proved too much to be ignored, Commissions of Enquiry have been appointed to go into the affairs of the councils concerned.

But, Commissions of Enquiry cannot provide an absolute or even the right remedy for the baneful disease; they cannot change people's characters. All they can do is to find out the cause or causes of a particular problem, apportion blame where necessary and appropriate, and, if they can, *suggest* possible remedies. If not properly handled, Commissions of Enquiry can do more harm than good. The real remedy lies with the people, the average men and women in the different communities. Even where they are themselves free from the evil, it is not enough for them to be indifferent to it. They must fight to kill it. That is why good men, Christians and other God-fearing people should go into all fields of public life with a determination, through their personal example, to convert and not be converted, to purify and not be polluted. By deciding neither to give nor receive bribes, and being courageous enough to ex-pose those with opposite inclinations, they can show a healthy example and give a good lead in the right direction.

There are indeed many good men among the councillors; men whose real purpose is to serve the people and not to look for private gains; men who are putting up a fierce battle even within the council walls against all forms of corruption. But they are all too few. Distressingly enough, many of them are beginning to feel disappointed and disillusioned, and are even beginning to wonder if their fight is worth while. The forces against which they fight seem all too powerful, both inside and outside the council halls. After all, the councils are democratic institutions whose decisions must be what the majority say; and if men of doubtful character are in the majority they will always *have their way* while the disinterested minority must be contented with the hardly effective privilege of *having their say*!

Such a role cannot be very encouraging to well-intentioned councillors, and has in fact led to a lot of potential and honest would-be councillors considering it best to stay clear. This is unfortunate. Viscount Samuel in his *Belief and Action* has this to say: 'If people of goodwill hold aloof from political organization, the state will sink into disorder; control will fall into worse hands, *and they themselves will be penalized.*' We could not do more than draw attention of those concerned to these statements.

In fairness to the majority of councillors, however, it must be observed that their inexperience in public affairs, in the art of debates and of administration is a great handicap to them. It is quite easy for clever rascals in the council to pull the wool over their eyes and lead them astray into supporting proposals which in effect merely feather the nests of particular persons. And this leads us to the invaluable practice of co-option.

(b) Co-opted Members

A principal feature in modern local government is the *Committee System.* Unlike organization, this is a most useful feature of the English Local Government which could be borrowed with utmost advantage. *Committees* are set up by the councils themselves and charged with specific responsibilities; and there are normally two types of them—*Standing Committees* and *Ad Hoc Committees.* To all these committees (with the possible exception of the Finance Committee) a council may co-opt persons who are not permanent members of the council, provided the number of such co-opted members does not exceed one-third of the total members of the committee concerned. This principle and practice of co-option has many advantages, the most outstanding of which is the opportunity it affords for 'bringing into the services of the public persons with suitable temperament and experience who do not desire to get too greatly mixed up in local politics'.[1] It is important that there should be present on our local government committees *and* councils, people with a fairly independent and neutral outlook, who can speak their minds without fear or favour, or even the fear of victimization in one form or another. It would not be safe enough to rely on the 'professional' (using the term in its good rather than derogatory sense) councillors who, judging from the present state of things, stand the risk of losing the next election as a result of intrigues and misrepresentations against them by their opponents. Not that they should be praised for being cowardly in the honest discharge of public duties, but one should not forget that they are human. Nor can the staff, who stand the risk of dismissal by a council if they are not careful, be expected to provide the healthy leadership, of which many of them are fully capable—no, not under the present system of their appointment and control.

It will be apparent from the preceding paragraph that we do not consider that it is enough to confine co-option or appointment of non-elected members to committees only. For such men as we have described above are also necessary in the full councils. Even if such people should be entitled to no votes (which might well be a desirable compromise with those who are yet shy of the co-optive principle) their views and presence might provide a very useful influence for the permanent and voting members.

The next thing which presents itself for consideration is the method of co-option. This is by no means an easy question. The Ordinance says that co-option should be done by the councils concerned. That is the legal position, which is not without its dangers. One danger is that in a council dominated by a political party there is the risk of

[1] Jackson, *Local Government in England and Wales* (p. 62).

116

the party co-opting only their political party members or sympathizers irrespective of whether there are others better qualified and more suitable for such appointment. Even in the unlikely event of it being possible to guard against such partisan consideration and favours, how can one be sure that the councils, with their limited experience, will be able to co-opt the right type of people?

In our quest for answers to these and other questions we were led into studying with interest the system of *aldermen* which exists in England. Under this system, councillors with long experience or even those who have never before been councillors though duly qualified, can be made *aldermen* and admitted into local government councils where they have as much right as any councillor in the daily affairs of the councils. In this way it is possible to retain the services of an experienced and good councillor who may happen not to secure re-election, or even to secure additional talent for the councils from other men of the community who have been outside the councils. To guard against an abuse by a political party using this to swell its own majority in the councils, some councils have a gentlemen's agreement whereby the number of aldermen with different political views is made proportionate to the strengths of the respective parties in the councils. An unfortunate thing now happening in the Eastern Region of Nigeria is that members of the old Native Authorities have in many cases been excluded from the councils for one reason or another. Had the practice of giving the old experienced councillors a position analogous to that of the English *aldermen* been in vogue *and disinterestedly applied*, it would have been possible to find a way of retaining the useful services of the experienced Native Administration councillors of proved ability on the new councils.

We do not, however, consider that the new councils should at this stage be trusted with making the appointments and co-option we have been discussing by themselves, unaided. This might well be one of those problems which the Central Government should help the local government bodies to solve, at least until the councils are much more experienced, with enough public-spirited men and women of good character and judgment serving on them. With the present Administrative Officers having direct responsibility and connection with local government bodies, they should be able to help the council in selecting the right type of persons for co-option to the councils and committees. This should not necessarily mean their making the co-option or appointments by themselves, for it would be effectively useful for them to suggest or submit to the councils a list of persons who, in their independent judgment, are worthy of co-option. Although this would not prevent dominating parties from selecting only their political favourites, it would at least ensure that as far as possible, people of character and ability are selected.

Another suggestion which might be made in conclusion to this section is that the Instruments establishing councils might make it obligatory for councils to co-opt certain central government officials, with specialist technical knowledge in their respective fields—e.g. the Provincial Engineer, the Education Officer, the Medical Officer, etc., on to committees where their expert advice can be easily placed at the disposal of the councillors. These busy officials need not, of course, be expected to attend every committee meeting, but only those which it is essential that they should attend, and even so they should have the right to decline attendance if other duties do not permit. Such a provision in the Instruments should not in any way be interpreted to mean an undue interference with the freedom and discretion of the councils, but only a means of ensuring that work is done properly.

(c) Traditional Authorities

We have early in this book shown that it would be ill-advised to exclude members of that class of citizens known as 'traditional rulers or authorities' from modern local government councils. It is gratifying to see that in the Gold Coast and the Western Region of Nigeria special provisions for the representation of this class of people on the new councils have been made—in some cases as much as one-third of the total number of seats being specially reserved for them. This was perhaps facilitated by the fact that in these places there have been well-established and generally recognized 'traditional or indigenous rulers'. But what about such places as the Eastern Region of Nigeria and other parts of Africa where there are no such indigenous rulers—at least not so many of them?[1]

As far as we know, in Eastern Nigeria, it is only in Calabar and Onitsha that special provision for indigenous or traditional authorities has been made for representation on the new local government councils. In the former place representatives of this class are elected from among themselves and on the councils are charged with special responsibility for matters affecting native law and custom, which, of course, includes such things as the disposal and alienation of land. The Obong of Calabar, however, though popularly crowned with pomp and splendour a few years ago, does not appear to have any special recognition in his person or office. There is no objection, however, to his being elected by other traditional leaders. But as a person who is traditionally well above all other traditional leaders in his *area of authority* he cannot, properly speaking, contest election with people who are but his lieutenants. One cannot help feeling that for a person like this provision should be made similar to that made for the Obi of Onitsha who, by virtue of his office and position, is the Chairman of the Onitsha Urban County Council. Onitsha has for a long time past had a recognized head—a king—(just as Calabar has) known as the *Obi*, an office which can only

[1] There is a definite move in the Eastern Region of Nigeria by the Government to give representation, where possible, to chiefs in the region. A Commissioner appointed from England is at present carrying out investigations. A Law has also been passed for the recognition of chiefs.

be held by members from particular families in Onitsha. The *Obi* as Chairman of the Council only attends on special occasions, leaving the actual day-to-day administration to an elected chairman. He is not only recognized as the Chairman of the Council, but also enjoys a regular honorarium from the funds of the Council. On the Council, too, is a special representation of the *Ndichies* who are lesser traditional authorities under the *Obi*.[1]

It is true that only in limited other cases can recognized authorities occupying the position of the *Obi of Onitsha* or the *Obong of Calabar* be found. Calabar and Onitsha are, of course, ancient towns with long established traditions. There are, however, the recently created and generally recognized and respected offices of *Mbong Ikpa Isong* (Clan Heads) among the Ibibios, persons whose sphere of influence may cover more than half of a whole County; and there are also traditional heads like the *Amanyanibo of Opobo* and the *Eze of Arochuku*, to mention only a selected few. These are certainly offices which it would be most unwise to ignore or, much more, to frustrate. They are authorities who might with advantage be recognized, respected and made use of even by the highest local government bodies.

Of lesser importance than the indigenous authorities of the order just mentioned are various age-grades and village heads. We have already seen (in the second chapter) what the position of the various age-grades is in the respective villages. The various village heads and leaders of age-grades are traditional authorities, whose spheres of influence are very limited indeed, scarcely extending beyond a single village, and very often confined to only one family or its extension. The fact that they are so many, are almost of the same status, have the same degree of authority, and,

---

[1] There is at present a strong public opinion that the Obi should be made *President* rather than *Chairman*, thus making his position purely constitutional or ceremonial. If this opinion eventually prevails, as is not very unlikely, it will be necessary to introduce amendments to the Ordinance which, at present, makes no provision for the office of President for the local government councils.

above all, have extremely limited spheres of influence, has been the chief cause in the past for their being ignored or, at best, regarded as of no political consequence.

Village Councils are in themselves limited to villages, inside which are these powerful and respectable indigenous authorities on whose shoulders the control and government of the villages largely, if not solely, previously rested—more strongly so before the British administration and limitedly afterwards. We tried to show in Chapter II that very often village government was carried out by means of what might be described as 'political divisions of labour' in that one authority might look after one aspect of village administration (what semblance of it there was) and another look after another. Where these different authorities existed there was usually one recognized village head over them all.

With the new local government systems, however, it is laid down that the strictly *localized* village councils should be constituted by election, which in itself is not a bad idea at all, except that it has in effect meant the exclusion of the respected and also strictly *localized* indigenous authorities, some of whom in the old days had the powers of life and death. Nothing, of course, prevents these traditional authorities from contesting election to the village councils just as anyone else can; but that feeling cannot be expected to go beyond mere expression. It would be expecting too much to expect village heads and other traditionally respected authorities 'to stoop to the indignity' of contesting election into *their* village councils side by side with 'disrespectful small boys' who tend to think that their education is a 'substitute for tradition'. Even in the unlikely case of their consenting to contest they stand the risk of being insulted and voted out by young people who may look upon them as a set of 'illiterate and unprogressive fools' whose days are no more.

Popular election then has kept the age-long village rulers out of direct touch with the daily administration of their own villages. The result has in most cases been unfortunate to the village councils and councillors. The councillors become unpopular and the smooth running of the councils has in many cases been impossible. There have been actual cases where bitter conflicts existed between the villagers backing their traditional rulers on the one side and the young councillors with a hardly appreciable number of outside supporters on the other. The conflict sometimes reached a stage where the councillors were ostracized by the whole community or punished with village fines and 'excommunication'—which in one case meant the extremely serious step in African custom of refusal by the village to join in burying dead relatives of the councillors—for their lawful performance of council duties. In some cases it was necessary for Government administrative officers to intervene in the interest of law and order. There were instances where the councillors themselves were compelled to appeal through the District Officers to the Government to see that official recognition was given to the traditional village leaders if the work of local government was in any way to progress smoothly. There was one rather peculiar but interesting instance where the Local or Village Council was virtually reduced to a position of obedient executors of the wishes and will of a group of traditional authorities known as *Otukpokolos* who were in no way members of the Council.

The above instances should clearly show that the village heads or authorities are not entirely without political consequence in their areas, even at this time. Their former authority and power may have very drastically diminished in the face of modern conditions, but their influence and respect among their people still live and linger. It is, however, reasonable to expect that wider progress in education will eventually, and almost imperceptibly, wipe out progressively outmoded traditional offices. But until that happens, what?

It is our well-considered view that the cause of local government would be better served with an official, if limited, representation of these traditional authorities in the village councils. Where there is a recognized Village Head, it might be well to provide that he or his representative should chairman village council meetings. Where there are powerful age-grades, they could be invited to send representative(s) to the village councils, provided such traditional representation does not exceed one-half or one-third of the elected members. There could be no harm at all in their presence on the councils, and it can be confidently said that they would scarcely oppose any progressive measures in the councils; and what is still more important, they and those they represent would be able to co-operate in carrying out the decisions and intentions of the village councils. There are healthy signs that, given an atmosphere of mutual respect, understanding and goodwill, the old village traditional authorities and the younger elected councillors could work hand in hand to the advantage and good of all.

(d) Chairmanship of Councils

In the Gold Coast and Western Nigeria—and indeed, as we have seen in Onitsha in Eastern Nigeria—the Head Chiefs of the Local, District and Divisional Council areas (the counterparts of District and County Councils in Eastern Nigeria) are normally made *ex-officio* Presidents or Chairmen of the Councils, and may attend council meetings only on special occasions, leaving the real work to an elected chairman. The wisdom of such a move could not be over-praised, and that is why we have stated above that we feel that the Ibibio Clan Heads, the Obong of Calabar, the Amanyanibo of Opobo, the Eze of Arochuku, and other people of similar status and position might be given similar ceremonial honour and functions. But, *it is best that the administrative chairmen of councils should be elected councillors answerable to the voters or electors.*

At this juncture we make bold to suggest that such artificial innovations like the office of *Mayor*, which was tried and abandoned not long ago in Lagos, should be introduced, if at all, with the greatest restraint and caution. Where a recognized traditional authority or political head exists, as indeed existed in Lagos, the choice of a 'commoner' to such an office at the expense of the indigenous dignatory, is bound to produce unpleasantness and disquiet even for the holders of the office. It would be better that recognized traditional leaders, where they exist, should perform any ceremonial and honorary functions where such are necessary. Where there are no such widely recognized and respected indigenous political heads, it would be better not to insist upon ceremonials and displays. In England itself the office of *Mayor*, with all that goes with it, is limited to a few specific local government areas.

(e) *Term of Office of Councillors*

There is hardly anything against the present practice, borrowed from England, whereby the normal term of office for councillors is three years, with one-third retiring and elected (if preferred) every year. It is best to say that this is a case where there may not be a general rule, and any arrangement might be made to suit individual cases or systems. One does, however, consider that three years should be about the longest life of a local government council before general election or retirement.

(f) *Politics in Local Government Councils*

The question whether or not 'politics' should be introduced into local government councils has evoked much discussion among many people. There was a time when the general trend of opinion was that party politics should be kept out of local government altogether. But that opinion hardly holds any ground nowadays, when the necessity of having political parties in local government bodies is almost generally accepted. What are the arguments?

Against: Since the general policy of local government bodies is laid down by the Central Government there is hardly any need for party politics. In Nigeria, for instance, the functions of local government bodies are specifically laid down and defined by the Ordinance and the Instruments establishing the respective bodies and it is not likely that there will be any fundamental differences in the methods of carrying out these functions as to necessitate dependence upon clear party principles. Most council business takes place in committees where it would be best not to display party politics. As parties are centrally controlled, and their policies centrally laid down, the introduction of party government into local government councils would make the councils lose their 'local' significance, since they would then be virtually controlled from the outside and too rigidly tied to national politics. Party politics would lead to endless squabbles in the councils, resulting in the creation of bad blood among members and the delay, possibly, of important work. It would exclude useful talents who have no party leanings from the councils; and finally, it is likely to make councillors sacrifice local practicabilities on the altar of party principles.

In Favour: Local government is but an aspect of National Government, and if the latter is run on party lines there is hardly any reason why the former should not be. Parties are necessary to stimulate interest in local government affairs among the otherwise lukewarm people, through propaganda and organization during elections. A council not run on party lines would be essentially inefficient, as there would be no Opposition to criticize and stimulate action. Lack of party system would result in personal rivalries among the councillors, who would lack discipline and control and be more interested in personal publicity than in constructive services.

The arguments appear balanced for both sides, although scarcely any of the points *for* or *against* can go completely unchallenged, but it is left to readers to form their own opinions. Some observations on one or two points may, nevertheless, be made here. First, the idea that since a national government which controls the local government bodies is run on party lines, local government bodies should also be run on similar lines. What, if—as is quite possible —the party controlling the national government is different from the one controlling, say, a rural district council? Is it not possible that one party would be playing against the other and even trying to sabotage or discredit the other's work, to the disadvantage of the general public—a situation that would scarcely arise if there had been no official parties in the local government councils? Secondly, there is the idea that those not attached to a political party would lack discipline, or be inefficient and self-seeking. It all depends on who is chosen. Presence or absence of politics cannot make good characters and no matter which is the case, bad men will make bad councillors and good men good councillors. With the modern means of publicity—the press and the radio—persons who know that their individual behaviour would be easily known and that they have no party cloak under which to hide in the event of personal misdeed and irresponsibility, are likely to be most careful in what they do. On the whole it would be in the best interests of the councils concerned that individual councillors should be able to express their honest and independent convictions in matters before them without any outside control which may result in one uttering words he does not sincerely believe. Lastly there is the argument that the question of party policy or principles cannot arise in local government administration because duties and functions are specifically laid down for local government bodies by the Central Government. That is true only up to a point. Certainly if, say, a question suddenly arose as to whether rates should be increased in order to build museums, or to give more assistance to secondary schools, or to give assistance to local farmers, a question of policy or principle is most likely to come in, over which there may be sharp division of opinion calling for party directive. But if, on the other hand, a market is to be improved it would scarcely be necessary to rely on a party principle in order to decide whether the improvement should start from the east or from the west end of the market.

If, however, a straight question were put to us as to whether we thought it desirable or advisable to practise party politics in our rural district and county councils we would unhesitatingly and emphatically reply 'No'. The experiment can be made, as at present, in the large townships where most people are likely to have at least a vague idea of what it means.

For a very long time in England, the mother of parliamentary government, politics were prudently kept out of local government administration, except in the highly cosmopolitan towns like London where, indeed, signs of strong party leanings first appeared clearly in 1934 at the instance of the Labour Party, which for many years afterwards continued to sponsor candidates on their platform for local government elections. The Conservative Party did not follow suit until a few years ago. Even so, there is a strong section of opinion which is still not convinced about the wisdom of the practice. That is in England, in England with centuries of experience in parliamentary government; in England where nearly the whole population know what political parties are and stand for.

In the rural areas of most African countries, none but the very few educated people really know what party philosophies are. They can only distinguish one party from another according to which of the people they know belong to which. Because of this appalling ignorance about political principles or philosophies in the rural areas, it would be more than confusing to introduce politics into local government elections there. Besides other arguments which can be advanced in support of this statement, the people are so much in need of development that our local government bodies need harmony and freedom from political strife in their daily duties. There are scarcely any functions from the list assigned to local government bodies—except perhaps in points of emphasis—which require political principle or policy to carry out. Men of ability, adequate education and intelligence are so few in the rural areas that it would be highly undesirable to exclude from the councils those willing to serve because of politics.

There is no doubt but that councillors as human beings in the modern world must have political sympathies—but the interests of the councils and of the localities affected would be best served if individual councillors kept their political views to themselves, and did not parade them on the floors of the councils.

CHAPTER IX

ADMINISTRATION OF LOCAL GOVERNMENT

(a) Co-ordinating Agencies

WE have not in the preceding chapter discussed as we should have done, the constitution of our 'novel' Co-ordinating Agencies—if indeed it is right to describe them as novel. That was because we felt we could discuss both the administration and constitution of the Agencies together with greater convenience. Questions of local government are so interwoven and so closely related that it scarcely matters where a particular subject is discussed in a book of this nature, so long as it is discussed at all. That also explains why occasional repetition and cross-references are almost inevitable in a book on local government.

It should have been clear from earlier chapters what our aims are as regards the constitution of the Co-ordinating Agencies. These bodies could be constituted in much the same way as a Joint Committee set up by local government bodies, in that members would be elected from among the members (elected and co-opted) of the lower, i.e. District, Councils. There would, however, be fundamental differences between the position of Joint Committees and the Co-ordinating Agencies. In the case of the former (Joint Committees) members are *appointed* and not necessarily *elected* by the member-bodies and the members so appointed take their seats on the Committees merely as representatives of—if it would not be even better to say *delegates* from—the bodies from which they come. For the Co-ordinating Agencies, the members, though possibly *elected* from and by the District Councils, would not have the status of delegates from these latter councils. *They would be both representatives of the District Councils and of the people at large,* and should have the *independence, freedom and power of initiative and action* that a *representative of the people* is expected to have. Copies of the minutes of the Co-ordinating Agencies might be sent to the District Councils regularly for information, but the District Councils should have no power of discussing the minutes in such a way as to imply that they had powers other than those of an ordinary citizen to criticize and direct the Agencies. They might express general feelings on the minutes which might serve the representatives as a useful index of public opinion on the work of the Agencies. The District Councils, then, would virtually be electoral colleges for the Co-ordinating Agencies. The representatives would have the right to tell the District Councils in person what is happening at the Agencies just as an elected member would tell his constituency. The District Councils whose duty it is to provide the funds needed by the Co-ordinating Agencies should have a right to this first-hand information on the work and progress of the Agencies and that may well be one of their real advantages for having to act as electoral colleges for the Agencies.

The chairman of a Co-ordinating Agency need not necessarily be a member of a District Council and could, indeed preferably, be independently appointed, for his personal skill and qualities, by the Central Government. He should nevertheless be responsible to the Agency which should be given powers, by a reasonable majority *and* subject to the approval of the Minister, to remove him from office for incapability or misconduct. His appointment need not be permanent, although he might be given a reasonably fair remuneration to make him give enough time to his duties, which would include the supervision of the day-to-day administration and working of the Agency.

The staff of the Agency should be well qualified and selected so as to be able to carry out their daily duties as independently as possible in much the same way as the civil servants of the Central Government. The elected members of the Co-ordinating Agencies would thus have lighter duties to perform than even the District Councillors are expected to do, and would, therefore, not find their duties on the Agency too strenuous or burdensome to cope with, in addition to their duties on District Councils from which they were selected. We think that meetings of the Agency should take place much less frequently than those of the District Council—say twice or thrice a year, or at the request of the chairman in case of emergency.

The functions of the members of this Agency would be, in the first place, to scrutinize and approve the estimates of the Co-ordinating Agency, which should be prepared and submitted by the permanent staff in consultation with the Chairman. They would also lay down policies for the permanent staff to follow, and *generally* concern themselves with the discipline of the staff. Their meetings, subsequent to the 'budget' one, would be concerned with such routine matters as receiving and considering periodical reports from the staff on the work of the Agency, making constructive criticisms, laying down new policy or giving new directives and, of course, considering any supplementary expenditure which may be necessary. *Financial control should be their absolute responsibility.*

The conditions of service for the staff would be generally determined by the Minister, and follow a national pattern. In addition to what is done in this respect by the Chairman of the Agency, the supervision of the daily conduct and work of the staff would also be generally, but only generally, carried out by Central Government Officials in the area, to whom the Minister might wish to delegate such and other functions. General discussion of appointment and other matters connected with the employment of local government officials follows in the next section.

(b) Staff

The importance of an efficient and contented staff is so great for the success of local government that it is advisable to discuss their appointment and other matters connected with their employment here before passing on to something else. For our purpose, this is much more relevant than trying to discuss the actual functions of the staff concerned. For the necessary success to be achieved the staff must be of highest quality: they must be well qualified educationally for their work, be of good ability and of very high character and integrity. A member of the staff having these and other obvious qualities and qualifications requires for his part good conditions of service, security of employment and an opportunity to develop his personality to the full—which means that he should have enough scope for individual initiative and enterprise in the discharge of his duties.

In the Eastern Region of Nigeria the English practice in this respect, whereby the appointment and control of local government staff are the direct and sole responsibilities of the Authority concerned, is followed.[1] (As in many other matters, this is a case in which the vast differences in conditions and circumstances existing between the two parts of the world appear to have been given insufficient weight.) The different Councils appoint their own staff and determine the salaries and other conditions of service for such staff. The Central Government, contrary to what used to be the case with the immediate predecessors of the new Councils, scarcely does anything to direct or advise these new Authorities on what should be done, the obvious excuse being that to do so would be, or appear to be, an attempt to perpetuate the old practice. Apart from the fact that the Regional Authority—like the Minister of Health in England, for instance—retains the power to approve the appointment and dismissal of certain categories of staff the Councils have absolute control over their staff. The result of the experiment so far cannot be said to be wholly satisfactory. The wrong appointments—and unfair dismissals—by some authorities and the dangerous disparity in conditions of service for the staff existing between one authority and

[1] But see Appendix C.

another cannot be passed as good auguries for the future of local government.

It has been mentioned earlier that local and parochial loyalties in most parts of the new territories are as yet all too strong to be resisted or even ignored in the interests of wider issues. This state of affairs has not been without its influence even in such things as the appointment of staff by local government bodies. That is why, among almost all the councils, there is such strong tendency to appoint only 'a son of the soil' to any important post that may be available with a local government council. This has often led to disputes among the councillors themselves as well as to the appointment of unqualified, or inadequately qualified, staffs at the expense of much better qualified persons from elsewhere who might have applied for the posts concerned. As these lines are written, there is information that one County Council is on the verge of collapse and dissolution because of serious disputes over this question of staff appointment, the various sections making up the County having each claimed that their own man should be appointed to one responsible post or another. This, of course, was impossible and a crisis came, but hardly surprisingly in the face of prevailing circumstances.

It is a thing to be desired that a good 'son of the soil', armed with his good local knowledge of the people and conditions, should be appointed if available by a local government body to such important offices as that of the Council Secretary or Town Clerk. But this is a wish that can hardly be satisfied in most cases without some sacrifice —in some cases very serious sacrifice—of efficiency, quality and good administration. For very few councils can boast of men from and in their areas, well qualified for the great and onerous responsibilities that must needs fall upon the shoulders of a modern executive officer of a local government council. At the same time, there may well be places where it would be best to have a purely disinterested stranger as a chief executive officer of the local government council. To try here to adduce arguments in support of how forcefully true, under many African social conditions, is the saying that a prophet is without honour in his own country would be to digress too wide from our point.

There is again the question of disparity in conditions of service arising from the Councils' independent powers to settle these. It would be difficult to expect a staff in one District Council, who knows that he is being paid much less than his counterpart in another District, to be efficient, happy and contented. That would certainly be unnatural. But the unfairness, with all its undesirable consequences, is bound to persist so long as people with different outlook and temperament serve on the different councils, and the relative wealth of the Authorities is different. The healthy practice in England whereby local authorities when making appointments and settling conditions of service 'not only watch each other's practice, but also have regard to the civil service conditions as far as these are applicable'[1] has as yet taken no firm root with our new local government bodies. People have sometimes suggested that a local authority should pay its staff what salaries it can afford. If this implies a justification to underpay or underrate its staff, then it is an unfair and unwise argument. Labour has but one market; and a local authority has no greater right to expect a man whose services are worth £600 elsewhere to agree to serve the authority for a payment of £300, any more than such authority would expect a firm dealing in ambulances whose market value is £600 each to sell it to the particular authority for just £300 because such authority cannot afford more. A local authority like a private individual should have the services or commodities which it can afford or go without them—except in the rare cases of its being lucky enough to see owners of the services or commodities in question willing of their own accord and with the full knowledge of what they are doing to give them at less than the market value. It does very often happen

[1] Jackson, *Local Government in England and Wales.*

134

that somebody looking for a job is willing to accept any offer made by an employer, but once he has settled in the job there is always the possibility of his becoming discontented unless his conditions of service are brought into line with what his counterparts in the same or other employment enjoy. This is exactly what is now happening with the staff employed by local government bodies in some parts of Africa who know that their next-door neighbours in other authorities are receiving fairer treatments than they themselves; and that is why one can rightly feel that the Central Government is in duty bound to see that minimum, if not uniform, standards of pay are laid down for the various grades of local government employees.

We suggest below steps which might be taken with good results, to provide, as far as general conditions allow, the new local government bodies with efficient and contented service.

Appointment and Control of Staff. The appointment of important and highly paid staff, requiring the possession of special qualifications for their job, might be done by an independent public commission, such as exists for the central civil service. With such a body in existence, any council needing such staff would have to apply to the Commission, either direct or through the Ministry or some other approved channel. The post or posts would then be advertised, and the Commission would interview the prospective candidates. After the interview the Commission might do either of two things. It might be empowered to make final appointments on behalf of the authority concerned; or it might, instead, make recommendations to the local authority concerned, which would then choose from among a group of candidates with whose qualifications the Commission would have been satisfied. An alternative to an independent commission as just envisaged would be a sort of Joint Appointments Committee (which might even be derived from the Co-ordinating Agency) set up for or by the various local authorities of a given area. Such a Committee would set about its duty in just the same way as we have suggested above for a public commission.

While in the service of an authority, any staff, no matter how and by whom originally appointed, would be entirely responsible to the authority employing him and meeting the cost of his salary or wages. It is important that the appointment, and dismissal, of staff in certain categories should require the covering approval of the Minister—just as is the case at present. Such approvals by the Minister should not be formal but *real;* that is to say, the Minister should have the power to refuse approval, which in effect would mean annulling the council's decision in the matter before him.

The procedure suggested in the preceding two paragraphs would ensure that the councils employ at least the best people available, remove one dangerous bone of contention among the councillors, and provide reasonable security for the senior members of the staff, but all this without taking away from the councils concerned their right of control and discipline over their own members of the staff.

Conditions of Service. We have stressed the desirability of having fairly uniform conditions of service in local government in any one country or region of a country. To achieve this it might be necessary for the Minister to evolve a sort of standing guide for the authorities. Otherwise, a sort of Joint Committee or even a Regional Local Government Association might be set up to see about the settlement or determination of suitable conditions of service which, of course, must be subject to the Minister's approval before becoming effective. The Joint Committee or Regional Local Government Association would be a sort of Local Government Whitley Council on which both the employers and the employed would be represented.

It must here be acknowledged that there might be real difficulty in settling general conditions in such minor things as leave, since there may well be differences in times and length of employment of staff between the various authorities. It might be wisest to leave such minor matters to the individual authorities, while matters like salaries, retiring benefits and pensions, and so on, are determined centrally in any of the ways we have suggested above.

Security. Nobody can be happy in any business or occupation in which his future is uncertain and insecure. Members of local government service cannot, of course, be exceptions to this rule. In a previous section mention was made of how reasonable security could be procured for the senior members of the service by means of the Minister having to approve their appointment and dismissal. But this practice would not apply to the junior members of the staff whose fate is left entirely in the hands of councillors. Their different positions notwithstanding (one wonders if the difference is appreciable now that local government elections are conducted on political lines), local government councillors should have no more right to control the permanent staff than members of the national parliament have to control members of the permanent civil service. That is why one may be very much inclined to endorse the practice obtaining in Ireland, for example, where the chief executive officer is solely responsible for the control of the junior staff under him. (See next chapter.)

As in the civil service any person employed in the permanent service of a local government body should serve a probationary period after which he would be *confirmed* in his appointment. Confirmation in appointment should imply that he cannot be dismissed at will from his employment except in certain cases of gross misconduct. His probationary period should be long enough to enable his ability to hold his office to be properly assessed. His subsequent inefficiency should not, *de facto*, constitute a ground for dismissal but a deterrent to further advancement. If after confirmation a council should decide to remove a staff member for inefficiency or any other reason, such an individual should be entitled to some retiring benefits and/or compensation. All these would prevent the present unsatisfactory situation whereby a council can dismiss its staff at any time no matter what his length of service.

Mobility. Arrangement should exist whereby an employee could be transferred from one authority to another without any loss of pension rights. An employee's pension rights on transfer might be preserved by a system of what is known in England as 'transfer value', whereby the authority from which a member of staff is transferring pays to the new employing authority full value of pension rights that the member of staff might have earned while in its employ, so that on final retirement the last authority employing him pays to such an employee full retiring benefits for *his whole period* of service. Such a practice one feels would be to the mutual advantage of both the employer and the employed. For an employee who is made to remain in one locality all his life, serving the same employers and moving about in the same environment, is likely to become 'stale' and narrow in outlook. Occasional change from one environment to another and experience in and with other places and people can have healthy effects on a man's efficiency and outlook in occupations connected with social administration such as local government. Apart from this, an opportunity for such mobility would provide an employee with additional means of security and chances for advancement. It would also save the council concerned from serious difficulties with an employee who cannot be easily removed. It sometimes happens, for reasons which neither party can readily explain, that a council and its senior staff find themselves unable to get on peacefully and well together. If an efficient and good member of staff is not to lose his job without justifiable reasons, or if the efficient administration of the council is not to be compromised, the only pleasant solution appears to lie in the transfer of the individual concerned to another place. To facilitate this process of transfer a system of 'provincialization' has been suggested by some people. By it, the whole of the local government staff in an administrative province (as known in the colonial territories) would be regarded as being in a sort of pool and liable for transfer from one area to another as the need arises. Provided that the obvious difficulties which are likely to lie in the way of this practice are successfully cleared (and this does not appear impossible) one would honestly endorse this idea of provincialization.

A word or two on the mutual relationship between council and staff, and we are done with this section. One striking feature which greatly impresses a visitor to England about the English system of local government is the very cordial relationship which exists almost everywhere between council and staff. This relationship is based on mutual confidence and respect. The Town Clerk for instance is at once the leader and servant of his council. He is not just regarded as a servant whose principal and sole duty is to obey orders from the council as his employer. On the contrary, the council, although his employer, always acknowledges and appreciates the special qualifications and experience which its Town Clerk has, and is never reluctant or ashamed to lean on him for leadership and advice, whenever it is necessary, in the interests of good business and administration. The Town Clerk, it is true, carries out the decisions and executes the policy of his council; and this he does very loyally and faithfully, even if he should happen to disagree with such a decision or policy. But there are very rarely cases where a Town Clerk seriously disagrees with his council; for he is normally afforded good opportunities to advise and in-fluence the decisions of his council, possibly during pre-liminary consultations and discussion before matters are formally brought to the council and settled. This is a commodity of local government administration worthy of 'export' to the new territories—and this in spite of our general and justified objections to reckless exportation of practices and systems!

To the new, and as yet inexperienced, members of the local government staff assuming heavy responsibilities one would like to suggest five general principles which may help them to success in their new positions:

1. They should realize and openly acknowledge their limitations, and then apply themselves resolutely to learning and improving themselves.

2. They should realize that in their positions as public servants, their duty is to serve the public cheerfully, loyally, and, where necessary, firmly but fairly.

3. They should try to wed themselves completely to their new responsibilities, which means that they should not only like but take a pride in these responsibilities.

4. They should not only be, but always appear to be, above-board in everything they do.

5. They must keep clear of partisan politics.

We do not know whether the above principles are full enough, but they would certainly be useful for a start.

(c) Committees

The use of committees in the day-to-day administration of business is a remarkably good practice in the English system. Since we have already touched upon the committee system in the previous chapter it will not be necessary to discuss the point here again at length. All that might be reiterated is that people most capable in the respective fields should be appointed to committees concerned with such fields, and where a council is lacking in internal expert advice liberal resort should be had to the co-option of suitable persons from outside. For the Finance Committee it might be in the interests of smooth administration to have, as is the practice with many councils in England, the chairman or deputy of every other committee of the council (particularly standing committee) serving on the Finance Committee in addition to any other person.

(d) Central Government Administrative Officers

These central government officials have been mentioned more than once in the preceding chapters. It has particularly been suggested that, where that has not already been done, some of the powers of control retained by the Central Government might, with considerable administrative advantage, be delegated to them. The importance of this suggestion lies in the fact that these officers are nearer the spot and closer to the people and councils than the distant and busy Minister. In addition, they enjoy general popularity and confidence among the people, and it would be useful not to withdraw their experience and influence from local government administration which only until yesterday had been their direct responsibility.

It is, however, clear that whatever a District Officer's relationship with the new local government bodies in his area might be, such a relationship must be materially different from what it used to be with the old Native Authorities—it must be in consonance with changed conditions. 'Leadership, Guidance and Education from within' and *not* (as used to be the case with the old Native Administration system) 'Control and Direction from without' should be the governing motto of the new relationship. How the District Officer can reconcile this new role to the discharge of his delegated functions of control which has been advocated already would at first sight seem to be a bit difficult. The difficulty might further be increased by the fact that a District Officer in his Division is looked upon as the representative of the central government—an administrative arm and ears of the Executive Council or Cabinet—who should perhaps not get too involved in local government affairs. But whatever initial difficulty might exist cannot be insurmountable. Perhaps a little more explanation of how, it is believed, he could maintain his new relationship with the councils without prejudice to his position and other responsibilities, would help to clear the possible difficulties mentioned a short while ago.

'Leadership, guidance and education from within' should not necessarily mean that a District Officer need attend the council meetings in person. He should not in fact do this *except when his presence is absolutely necessary*, as when it is *urgently necessary in the interest of public order and good administration* that he should *advise* a whole council on specific matters. For example, a council might be operating or about to put into effect an unpopular, delicate or even inadvisable measure which, if not properly handled, could evoke strong popular opposition or even riot. Very often a District Officer is able to foresee such an outcome before the councillors themselves. He would be under obligation in such a case to attend a full meeting in which he can outline to the councillors his *personal* views and observations on the issue involved and advise them on what he himself feels might be done. Emphasis has been put on the words *advise* and *personal* to show that, whatever he tells the council at this stage, should not be taken as representing the official view—but only personal, friendly advice or suggestion. Should it be necessary later for him to exercise his special powers of control which might have been delegated to him by the Minister he should not, of course, set about the discharge of these powers with an attitude of 'I told you, but you would not take heed', but exercise the powers as if, in fact, he had never before told the Council anything about the measure they were undertaking. It is to be appreciated that, depending on the attitude and method of approach by the officer concerned, it may be hard to convince the councillors that his advice was not in fact instruction. It will call for all the tact and common sense of the officer concerned to win the confidence of his councillors so that whatever he does cannot be open to dangerous suspicions on the part of the councillors.

When and where it becomes necessary for the officer to attend a full council in order to render specific advice he should see that he leaves the meeting as soon as possible so as not in any way to hamper the council in their freedom of expression, thought and action. 'Leadership, guidance and education from within' would imply a position whereby the councillors and the District Officer would regard each other as friends with common aims to achieve a success—friends who not only trust but respect one another.   That would be a different relationship from what existed under the Native Administration system wherein the District Officer was always looked upon by the councillors as the 'master' whose role was to give authoritative instructions and orders which the councillors were bound to receive and execute even if it meant an indignant annulment and reversal of the latter's former decisions.   The new role then would mean periodical and informal discussion of affairs with leading members of the council and the senior staff of the Councils.   It should be the duty of the Chairman and/or the Administrative Secretary concerned to keep the District Officer regularly informed of the intentions and actions of the Council and to avail themselves of his advice.   It would be from such consultations that the District Officer would be able to know when to offer the general advice to a full council.

The salutary effects on local government administration of a District Officer and local government councillors and/or members of the staff having informal discussion and advice on local government matters—say over a cup of tea, a glass of beer, under a tree or in the car—can hardly be over-estimated.   A District Officer's influence and leadership through this way would be far more effective and far-reaching than authoritative orders—and here would surely lie a real advantage over the system of converting Administrative Officers into what is known in one area as 'Local Government Inspectors', a title which in itself is too authoritative and awe-inspiring to make a District Officer be freely regarded as a friend of the councillors and staff, and not a fault-finding authority with a big stick always in his hand!

However much a District Officer should have the right to know how important contracts are disposed of and what happens afterwards, he should not be too deeply involved in the financial administration of the council, beyond, possibly, general advice on the lines already suggested above. As a local representative of the Government or the Minister, important correspondence addressed to the Minister by a Council, on which the Minister would require advice and comments from the spot to be able to reach a fair and quick decision, should pass through the District Officer who would forward it with necessary comments and advice.

A situation such as has been depicted would not savour of a return to the old Native Administration system, which some inadequately informed quarters seem to fear. It would not interfere with the freedom, initiative and individual enterprise of the local government bodies which we, like others, strongly desire and advocate. It would simply make available to the local government bodies the administrative experience and qualifications which a professional administrator has—to the considerable advantage of all.

Now, it will be clear from the above that a District Officer who can successfully play the role we have described must require special qualifications, personal and academic. As this is not an appropriate place to discuss these, we can only refer our readers to Appendix A which contains further remarks on the position and future of Administrative Service.

(e) *Remuneration of Councillors*

This title is both sarcastic and misleading, and we have intentionally made it so. The principle of local government is that councillors should render free services to their Councils. They are expected to be content with the honour of serving their people as a sufficient reward for their trouble and labour. Local Government would be a farce without this spirit of 'voluntary service'. That is why one cannot help being disturbed when councillors start making unreasonable demands for financial allowances—remuneration—for their services to their Councils. It cannot be that such demands (speaking here particularly of Eastern Nigeria) are the result of an inherent lack of spirit for voluntary work among the people, for that spirit already exists in very great depth. Services for tribal and other cultural organizations are usually free and voluntary and, with a close and intimate knowledge of the working of these organizations, it can categorically be said that, given half the spirit and loyalty which exists among the members of these tribal and cultural organizations, our local government systems would be almost an unqualified success. The writer had, for many successive years, the great honour of serving as secretary to some of these organizations and remembers how very often members ungrudgingly stayed long hours at meetings (one meeting lasted from 5 p.m. until 4 a.m. the following day), travelled long distances to meetings, in sun and rain, hunger and thirst, and were prepared to sacrifice not only their time but their money and personal popularity and convenience in the cause and service of these unions and organizations, which they ostensibly believed to be necessary. Why then should the very people who have been making these big sacrifices for these unions and organizations be unwilling, or not quite so resolute, to give as much when called upon to serve the new Councils, without financial consideration for themselves?

The reason is not difficult to find. Local government service is still regarded as 'government' (which is synonymous with 'European') service; and the Councils with their powers of rating and taxation are judged to have money 'to spare'! A lot of councillors then do not understand why they should be required to render free services to these Councils as they did to tribal and cultural organizations whose source of income was the small contribution made by the individual members. A feeling of this nature is much more strengthened when councillors have to travel long distances to County Council Meeting where, most probably, they sit side by side with people they have never met before, speaking (as in one County at least) different languages and having more than imperceptible differences in basic culture.

In this latter case the meeting is neither *local* nor ethnic, and there is a complete absence of that most important prerequisite of local government—community feeling. In such circumstances it would be expecting too much to think that the councillors can have the spirit and feeling of intimacy, close mutual concern, and oneness—which constitute some of the strongest driving forces in tribal and other social organizations—making the members render such selfless services as we have noticed above. (Perhaps the sort of local government organization suggested in Chapter III would help in improving the situation!)

The Ordinance permits the Councils to determine and pay reasonable allowances to those councillors who travel fairly long distances to meetings. Most District and County councillors indeed travel long distances by road or water to attend meetings and other local government duties and are entitled to reimbursement of at least their travelling expenses. As a matter of convenience some Councils have fixed a sort of commuted and regular allowance which they pay to their councillors towards the meeting of these expenses. Without necessarily trying to make unfavourable inferences about the ability of the individual councils to determine what is a fair and reasonable allowance, one would suggest that the Minister should lay down guiding principles for the Councils to follow and know what in the Government's view is reasonable. This would avoid the demoralizing risk of councillors deciding what is later thought by the auditor as unreasonable, resulting in the councillors being 'surcharged'.

While fully accepting and encouraging the good principle of free service in local government work on the part of the councillors, one cannot help suggesting that care should be taken not to allow this principle to result in real personal hardships or financial losses to the councillors. The principle worked so well and for so long in England because of the existence of a group of well-to-do leisured gentlemen able and willing to give voluntary services for local government administration. Such a class of people scarcely exists in any of our developing territories—and even in England the position is radically changing in the face of modern requirements and the complexities of local government administration, coupled with the introduction of party politics into local government administration. Some financial assistance, then, is inevitable. Conditions should be such that the poor and the well-to-do can feel encouraged to serve as councillors, but without making local government service lose its essence of voluntary service or even making people consider it a source of additional income if not a remunerative career.

An allowance to a local government councillor should be 'reasonable', one feels, if it is enough to cover his travelling expenses with a small margin for refreshments while attending meetings, and the small official correspondence that he may find it necessary to undertake. Presidents and Chairmen of Councils might be given enough but not generous allowances for entertainment and loss of time for their extra responsibilities. We do not know whether it would be wise or desirable, at this stage of local government development, to introduce the practice adopted in some countries of paying councillors, who have to leave their work to attend council meetings, a small allowance for loss of earnings. Normally such an allowance should not exceed £1 per sitting.

CHAPTER X

OTHER SYSTEMS

A NY system of local government should reflect the special characteristics and local circumstances—historical, environmental, etc.—of the country in which it is practised. The previous chapters have been devoted to a discussion of what sort of system might be most suited to African conditions. In doing so frequent references were made to the English system which has been the main source of lessons for those British colonial territories which have so far adopted the more advanced forms of local government. The main purpose of the present chapter is to have sketchy glances at the practices of local government adopted by old countries other than England. This course is taken in the honest belief that some acquaintance—no matter how sketchy, as this chapter is necessarily going to be—would be useful for the new countries trying to evolve their own systems of advanced local government.

The success of any form of local government will depend on how good and efficient its administration is, much more than in the actual organization. In the discussion, therefore, which follows we shall look at these other systems more from the administrative angle than from the organizational one. We have chosen for this very brief discussion the Irish, French, Swedish and American systems.

(1) THE IRISH SYSTEM

The Irish system is of particular interest to us. Ireland, readers will remember, formerly had almost the same colonial status as Nigeria, the Gold Coast, Tanganyika, etc., now have. Like most of these places she started her experiment in local government by borrowing largely from the English system. But she later found this to be not quite suitable for her own peculiar circumstances and had to introduce something more consonant with her administrative needs. Naturally, she turned her attention to other countries to see if there could be something there not present in the English system which might be adapted to her own conditions and requirements. American systems were found to contain some material which she might usefully adapt.

By the *Irish County Management Act*, local government administration is left largely in the hands of County Managers who are appointed by the Minister on the recommendation of Local Appointments Commissioners. These County Managers hold office for life, or until they are removed from office or themselves resign; but the Minister retains the right to revoke the appointment of any County Manager whenever he thinks fit. Once appointed, the County Manager becomes solely responsible to the Council he is to serve. His salary is fixed by the Minister of Local Government, though the cost is borne by the Council or Councils concerned. The position of the County Manager *vis-à-vis* his employing Council or Councils (for one County Manager may serve more than one County) is interesting. He is, technically speaking, responsible to the Council, but the Council has only general supervisory powers over his work and conduct. Only in cases where the County Manager clearly omits to carry out specific duties can the Council require him to perform such duties, provided they are lawful and funds are available. Should it be necessary to suspend or dismiss the County Manager, his employing Council can only, by a two-thirds majority vote, make recommendations to this effect to the Minister of Local Government, on whom rests the final word. The Council as such has no control over any other member of its staff. Appointments, control and general conditions of service affecting all other members of local government staff fall within the absolute responsibilities of the County Manager; also such powers as the granting or withholding of public assistance to particular individuals as well as the prosecution or non-prosecution of any particular persons.

The Council, however, is not without its powers and rights. They have absolute control over the finances of the Council. They scrutinize and approve the annual estimates submitted by the Manager and the amounts approved *cannot* be exceeded without their consent and approval. The Council alone can borrow money or levy rates and they alone can make, amend or revoke bye-laws. The Act, in short, specifies what it calls 'Reserved Functions' for the Council and 'Executive Functions' for the County Manager.

Committee System. A Council may appoint committees to which it can delegate some of its supervisory functions and other *reserved* powers. Delegation of *executive* functions to committees is the concern of the County Manager, but subject to the consent of the Minister. Non-County Council members may also be co-opted to certain committees.

Organization. The Administrative County, which is either a County for which a Council is elected or a County Borough (i.e. Municipality), is the principal unit of local government. A County is made up of one or more county districts which may be either urban or rural (otherwise known as urban sanitary district or rural sanitary district).

(II) THE FRENCH SYSTEM

The system in France is quite different from both the English and Irish systems. Indeed, a study of the French system of Local Government (and administration) constantly reminds one of common features in that system of Local Government known as Native Administration (or Indirect Rule) now being superseded in some, but still in vogue in other, African territories under British Rule. In both the French system and African Native Administration systems local government units are but units of central government administration; in both central government officials play leading and very often decisive roles in the actual administration of the councils; in both certain decisions of the councils require approval or confirmation by a central government official before they can be put into force. More analogies could be drawn, but it would not, of course, be right to assume that they are more than thin analogies—no one should think that a study of the one system only can lead to the understanding of the other. Though the features in one can easily remind a student of the features in the other, they are in actual practice substantially and naturally different. For example, whereas in the Native Administration systems of Africa most, if not all, councillors are normally appointed or nominated by the central government, in the French system councillors are all elected. Again, whereas in the Native Administration system, central government officials are supposed (indeed expected) to act *indirectly* and in an 'advisory' capacity, in the French system these officials may act directly and authoritatively with and against the councils. In short, against any analogy that can be drawn between the two systems one can find fundamental differences such as the two just mentioned.

The principal units of Local Government in France are the *Communes* and the *Départements*, the latter being made up of a number of the former. It would be a little inaccurate if not misleading to quote direct counterparts of these bodies in the system of local government as known in England or even in Eastern Nigeria. Although *communes* with populations as small as fifty inhabitants can be found in France, yet it would be wrong to compare them to the English Parish, for a *commune* is a more responsible body than a Parish; but still cannot be properly compared with a District Council. Coming to the *Département*, the analogy is still more difficult to find in the English system, although considering the position and powers of the *Prefect* who is in charge of the Department, one would be tempted to compare it with an Administrative Province in Africa, with the Resident or Provincial Commissioner taking the place of the Prefect; but only if the Resident or Provincial Commissioner had a Provincial Council with elected members who were responsible for decisions which the Resident or Provincial Commissioner would be expected to execute, subject to his reserved powers to challenge the legality of the Council's decision or to advise the Minister, who is the tutelage authority, on the behaviour and actions of the Council.

Communal Administration. The elected body in charge of a *commune* is known as the *Conseil Municipal.* Its executive head is the Mayor, also an elected person. The Mayor, though not directly appointed by the Central Government, is required to perform certain duties for the central government and this, in fact, makes him a state official. With the exception of certain things of purely communal interest a *commune* cannot act without the approval of the Prefect or Sub-Prefect. The Mayor is directly subordinate to the Prefect who has the power to suspend him for a limited period if the Mayor should prove inefficient or insubordinate. The Minister of the Interior, upon the recommendation of the Prefect, can suspend a Mayor for a longer period than the Prefect can, and may in very serious cases dismiss the Mayor from office.

It is within the Prefect's powers, too, to dismiss individual members of the *conseil municipal* (which reminds one of the powers of the Resident or Provincial Commissioner in Africa to dismiss individual councillors under the Native Administration System) and a whole *conseil* can be dismissed as a body for inability to function or even abuse of power. (Cp. the powers of the Minister of Internal Affairs in Eastern Nigeria to dissolve a council, *vide* Appendix B.)

By means of what is known as the *Syndicat Intercommunal,* different *communes* with the approval of the *Conseil Général* (see below) can join together to provide services which they cannot individually provide. Each such *commune* is entitled to send equal representatives to serve on the *Syndicat*. It is also possible for a small and weak *commune* to ask to be joined with a bigger and richer *commune*, subject to certain safeguards.

Departmental Administration. Conseil Général is the elected body for the Department. The executive head is the *Prefect*.

The position of the Prefect in the Department as a whole is one of very considerable responsibility and authority. He is the personal representative of all the Ministries in his Department. He is 'the hierarchic superior of all state officials in the Department no matter what their seniority or status'. (Chapman: *Introduction to French Local Government*.)

His tutelage powers over Local Government bodies are however confined to the *communes* and do not extend to the *Conseil Général*. Indeed, the *Conseil Général* is so important a body in the State that its tutelage authorities are the Ministers of the Interior and of Finance, although, of course, these Ministers are usually advised by their personal representative, the Prefect. 'An individual member of the *Conseil Général* can only be dismissed by that body and then only if he has failed to attend meetings on two consecutive occasions without good reason.' (Chapman: *Introduction to French Local Government*.) The authority of the Prefect over a *Conseil Général* 'is one of personal persuasion and not of legal superiority', which means that the personality of the individual Prefect concerned must play no inconsiderable part. It is, however, within the powers of the Prefect to challenge before the *Conseil d'Etat* (an Administrative Court), and within a specified time, the legal validity of decisions taken by a *Conseil Général*.

The Committee System. The Committee system, an almost indispensable institution in the English system of Local Government, is not popular in France, which should not be surprising judging by what has been said about the position and functions of the Chief Executives of the local government bodies. This should not, however, be taken to mean that Committees are entirely unknown, except in our own understanding of the term. It is possible for the *Conseil Municipal* to appoint Committees which may be entrusted with certain functions, but that is left entirely to the *Conseil* concerned.

There is, however, for the *Département*, something which can appropriately, though somewhat reservedly, be compared to a standing committee known in the British systems. It is what is known as *Commission Départementale*, a body made up of elected members of the *conseil* with the duties, among other things, of:

(i) examining the Prefect's accounts every month;
(ii) examining beforehand the Prefect's draft budget with a view to submitting a report on it to the full council when the budget is formally presented;
(iii) examining the agenda prepared by the Prefect for a full meeting of the *Conseil* and reporting thereon.

The *Conseil* can, of course, assign (within the law) certain other powers to the *Commission*.

Judicial Control. Cases of dispute or disagreement between the executive and the elected bodies, or about the rightness and legal validity of decisions and actions by the *Conseils*, the Executives or other officials are determined by the *Conseil d'Etat*, an administrative court. Appeals to this court can be made either by the Mayor, the Prefect or the *Conseils* themselves. Local authorities can also appeal to the Minister against the actions or decisions of the Prefect.

(*Note:* An interesting thing, worthy of notice by African nations seeking systems, is that France is a much larger country than England. It is also less industrialized than England; or to put it in other words, has more widely scattered rural populations. This is true also of African territories. With poor communications and preponderantly illiterate populations existing in these territories, one is tempted to think that the following two needs cannot be overlooked, if the aims of local government mentioned at the beginning of this book are not to be compromised:

(i) A fairly decentralized system of local government administration; and
(ii) The need for central government officials to provide control and guidance to local government bodies, particularly in the rural areas.

The reasons for these suggestions need hardly be stressed. With poor communications, centralization of control is bound to lead to delays and inefficiency, and with the majority of the people illiterate, local government bodies cannot be expected to find their way without expert guidance.)

(III) THE SWEDISH SYSTEM

The Swedish system is also interesting to look at. Here there are the *communes* which are, in varying degrees, subordinate to the County, in which they are situated. The County Council meets at least once a year. A rather curious feature is what is known as a Standing Administrative Committee which can carry on when the County Council is not in session. The County Council has a local legislative and taxation authority, and serves also as an electoral college for elections to the Senate. The Prefect (or Governor) who is in charge of each County is appointed by the Central Government and enjoys a salary almost equal to that of a Cabinet Minister. His functions are two-fold: (1) He acts as the Central Government representative as well as performing central government functions, such as the issuing of passports. (2) He acts as the chief executive of the Councils, and in this capacity may attend meetings and propose motions although he himself has no vote.

(IV) THE AMERICAN SYSTEM

An important feature in the American local government system is the predominance and importance of municipalities or cities. These are growing very fast both in number and in strength. As might be expected there are many different forms of local government administration in America; but of these three are the most popular and widely known, and these are the 'Mayor-and-Council System', the 'Commission System' and the 'City-Manager System'.

(a) *The Mayor-and-Council System.* Under this system there is an elected council and an elected mayor. The powers of the mayor depend on whether the mayor is 'strong' or whether he is 'weak'. The 'weak mayor' system is said to be the original form of municipal government in America, and under it the position of the mayor is mainly honorary, since the mayor is more or less an administrative figurehead. The 'strong mayor' system on the other hand is one in which the mayor has much wider and more effective powers in the administration of his municipal departments, while the Council confines itself to general legislation and close-watching. The powers of a 'strong mayor' range from the control of staff, which includes powers of appointment and dismissal, to the submission of budgets and programmes to the Council; from being chairman at council meetings and taking full part in the deliberations, to having the powers of veto, which can only be reversed by a two-thirds majority vote. He directs the municipal actions and is the ceremonial head of his city. He enjoys a very high salary and his term of office may range from one to five years. This system operates principally in the large cities, but its popularity is extending.

(b) *The Commission System.* This system has a certain amount of resemblance to the British system whereby all the councillors are administrators as well as 'legislators'.

Under it each councillor has some specific field of responsibility by means of what is very much akin to the English
committee system. One other feature of similarity between
this and the English system is the practice of 'staggering'
the terms of office for councillors, so that all councillors do
not retire at once, thus ensuring continuity of administration.

(c) *The City-Manager System.* This is the system whereby
local government administration is run on business lines.
Under it, there is an elected council and a professional
manager. This manager, unlike a mayor, is not elected
but appointed by the Council. The elected councillors,
like a board of directors in a business concern, lay down
general policy by means of council decisions, leaving the
day-to-day administration entirely in the hands of their
appointed manager. In a way the position of the city-
manager is similar to that of an English Town Clerk in that
he, as the chief executive officer, is not a member of the
council but an employee whose duty is to carry out loyally
and faithfully the decisions of his council, whether he likes
them or not. Like the English Town Clerk again, he is a
person of considerable experience which, in turn, makes
him a highly respected person even among his own employers who, whenever the need arises, do not hesitate to
turn to him for advice in matters of a technical nature.

(This is the system from which Ireland has largely
borrowed—*supra.*)

General

We have mentioned the importance of municipalities in
the American system of local government. Perhaps nothing
illustrates better the real degree of importance of this, than
the fact that in certain cities the salary of the mayor 'is equal
to or greater than the salary of the governor in the same
state'.[1] But this must not be understood to mean that the
municipalities are independent of the State in which they
are. They are not. As a matter of fact, none of them

[1] *American Government in Action*, p. 533.

enjoys as great a degree of independence as an English municipality. Even where the population of a municipality may be larger than that of all the remaining parts of the State, it is still subordinate to that State.

The American Counties

The term 'county', like many American words, has not an identical meaning with its counterparts in England. It is applied to rural areas of America and is what, in England or the Colonies, would be called a large rural district council, but without the powers and importance which such bodies enjoy in England. They have strikingly been described as the 'neglected children of the American government'. Like the *village councils* in some British territories, the powers of American counties are generally not clearly defined. Counties are looked upon as the agents of the State for giving effect to State laws. Like a Native Authority in a British colony they act as the agents of the State in the collection of certain taxes, and in return receive from the State a certain percentage of the taxes collected for use in meeting their own local administrative needs.

As would be expected, there is very strong public opinion in America favouring specific reforms in the American system of local government, particularly in the direction of granting more independence to the local authorities. In the same way the counties are generally thought to deserve far greater importance, respect and responsibility than they at present enjoy. But the nature of the American Constitution, like that of the French, makes reform not as easy as its advocates would like or expect.

America, indeed, is a peculiar country. She is, of course, the melting pot of all nations of the world. It will be seen from the above brief description of her systems of local government that a bit of practically all that we saw before is present in her systems—a bit of the Irish system (which, of course, was borrowed from America herself), a bit of the French, of the Swedish and, of course, of the

English. It would have been not only disappointing but also discrediting, if the American local government system had not been a melting pot of other systems, as the country herself has been of other nations—thus vindicating the opening sentence of this chapter.

CHAPTER XI

REFLECTION AND CONCLUSION

THIS book was started with a well-intentioned warning against reckless importation of other countries' systems of local government.   But this warning did not imply that eyes should be shut against anything good in one system which might be usefully adapted to another.   Only fools can fail to profit by other people's experience.   In an age in which the world has grown much smaller because of scientific discoveries, so that the different parts have become very closely inter-dependent, there are powerful trends towards, and in favour of, standardization in many things.   National sovereignties and, maybe, identities, are being surrendered in varying degrees by the different peoples in the interests of common standards which would clearly simplify relation-ships and mutual understanding.

In the colonial territories few things can retain their unsophisticated native appearance and features.   There is indeed already some fear of the people losing too much of their original native characteristics, with so much being borrowed from older countries of the world.   The English language, education, Christianity, democratic institutions, cultural tastes of different kinds, scientific inventions and a host of other things—things which the people love and cherish very much—have come from older civilizations, with which accident of history has brought the various territories into contact and by which the peoples' mode of life has been ordered and influenced for many years.   Most of these things have been received in their final or most developed stages without the necessity of the people having to go through the long and hard way of experience, trial and error.

It follows, then, that there can be nothing strange in the

newer countries drawing fully upon the experience of older ones in local government matters, although this should be done with much discrimination. Unlike a motor-car, political systems cannot be usefully imported in their *exact* patterns and forms. For unlike the solid earth on which the motor-car can be operated in whatever country to which it may be imported, the people among whom political systems operate have peculiar feelings, peculiar needs, and a past which cannot be ignored. In the different systems noticed in the last chapter, and in the English system to which constant reference was made in earlier chapters, historical and environmental needs and circumstances have had determinative effects.

A brief study of the history of English local government shows that its development has more or less centred round the provision of social services, which started with the administration of the *Poor Laws*. The method of local government administration has been consonant with the historical peculiarities of England. The degree of independence—not easily found in any other system in the world—which English local government bodies have enjoyed from the start has been a direct offshoot of England's singularly favourable political stability and internal security, which have been enhanced by both her geographical position and national characteristics. All these are factors which have made her system of local government, not unlike her other constitutional features, evolve through the centuries peacefully, flexibly; change and adapt itself to circumstances as they occur, without anybody or Government being particularly concerned or worried about the particular course it took. No need, for instance, has ever arisen for the Central Government as such to make any deliberate move to make the system follow any particular pattern in the overall interests of the State. At the same time people have always been readily available, with all the necessary qualifications and experience to carry out local government administration without the State having to intervene either in the interests of the staff or of the Council. Central control and supervision there has been, much more so in recent years, but there is still a wide measure of local initiative and independence within the frame-work of the very flexible British Constitution.

Turning to the French system one sees quite a different state of affairs. The French local government system did not undisturbedly grow 'peacefully and flexibly'. The pattern, still largely followed to-day, was deliberately set up by Napoleon between the years 1790 and 1800, actuated no doubt by contemporary political events—revolution, upheavals and confusion. These internal conditions then, as to some extent now, made it imperative that the State should take direct and close interest in the working of local government, and this has meant close supervision and control—indeed direct administration by the Central Government through the local *Prefect*. And, very much as the Native Administration units in a British colonial territory used to be, the French local government bodies are but direct units in the State's administrative machine. One simply needs to examine the conditions in France, even to-day, to realize that the British practice, exported to France, would hardly work.

About Sweden it is safe to say that her own system too is just the result of her peculiar circumstances.

As to America, it is hardly necessary to add to our brief remarks in the closing sections of the last chapter. The majority of readers will be acquainted with American history and social conditions, so as not to be unduly surprised about the diversity of the systems of local government administration noticed in that great country.

Finally there is Ireland, a part of the British Isles and a former British colony, where the English practice could not be successfully applied and a change had to be made.

What lessons can be learnt from all these by the new countries now busily concerned with local government development? Perhaps nothing really new or different from what has already been spotlighted in the preceding chapters. But we might remind ourselves here of a few striking lessons. The first is that whatever pattern of local government is adopted its success must *largely depend on how the actual administration is carried out.* That is the explanation of having the different devices in the different countries and places. A second lesson is that there may be certain aspects of administration operated in one country which may be quite useful to another, in which case it would not be wrong to borrow such features and *adapt them to local conditions and needs.* The County-Manager system of Ireland was a direct adaptation of the American City-Manager system, but notice how the practice was not simply transplanted in its entirety from America on to the Irish soil, but had to be modified to suit the local needs of Ireland. A third lesson is that even where something new has to be borrowed from elsewhere all that was good in the old system should be usefully retained. *A fourth lesson is that local government cannot be divorced from the central government and the actual relationship between the two must depend on the peculiar needs and circumstances of the country concerned.*

In the African colonial-territories systems of local government on modern lines are being introduced as a matter of plan and policy. This affords a healthy opportunity for comparing the experiences of older systems with the special needs of the different territories before arriving at a definite decision. This is the incalculable advantage which the younger countries have over the older ones—to have well-tried experiences to draw upon. It took some years of hard work and thought, for instance, to decide on the system to apply to the Eastern Region of Nigeria. Eyes were cast in many directions, particularly to other parts of Africa, before it was finally decided to adopt the English pattern. Although the resulting system might be said to be full of imperfections—which it is not too late to put right—it was perhaps the best that could be evolved under the circumstances of the time. It will remain a great credit to those responsible that something was done at all; it was a bold decision requiring plenty of courage and resolution, which immediately opened the way for others to follow. The Gold Coast and the Western Region of Nigeria have in turn largely followed the pattern set by the Eastern Region of Nigeria with, of course, minor modifications based on the experience of the Eastern Region to suit their own special circumstances.

Although, naturally, our attention was centred upon the Eastern Region of Nigeria, and England, for the arguments and illustrations used in this book, sight was never lost of the fact that our suggestions would also apply to most other countries of Africa. These territories, which have had the same experience of colonial administration and tutelage, are already in possession of common history with a common background and basis. The Indirect Rule system, for instance, born in Nigeria was not confined to that place but was applied everywhere in Africa under the British rule, with varying degrees of success. It is this fact which has made us firmly believe that what is good for one African territory can be found to be useful for the other. That is why it is not surprising that whenever something is success-fully tried in one part, eyes from other parts must be turned there for an example. For instance, before the reforms in the Eastern Region of Nigeria, a leading official was sent to Kenya and Uganda to study what was happening there to see what, if any, lesson could be usefully drawn for the Eastern Region. Since the reforms the Eastern Region of Nigeria has itself become the focus of eyes from other parts. This is just as it should be, for, besides the historical factor, there are a number of other fundamental factors common to most African territories: their social structures have much in common and their experiences have for some years past been much the same.

It is quite natural that a country under the British rule wishing to develop its own local government system should first of all turn its eyes to Great Britain, or a sister colony, for inspiration and guidance.   There is much in the English system to admire and emulate.   But there is also, for reasons which should by now have been obvious, a lot to disregard and avoid.   As far as our limitations permitted, we tried in the previous chapters to point to some of the features we thought fell within these two different categories. We cannot, of course, claim infallibility, and there may well be readers who are inclined to think differently in this respect.   If anything, our principal aim has been to encourage such 'discriminative' thoughts which can act as a deterrent to any dangerous tendency to swallow anything found in the English or, for that matter, any other system as being indisputably the best to adopt.

Local conditions and requirements—even as between one African territory and another—may be *similar* but can never be identical in two whole countries.   At the same time, experience of what happens in countries outside the Empire, studied in conjunction with what happens in England and other systems closer to us, could be of invaluable help in the proper assessment of values, in accordance with the respective needs of young inquiring countries.   Such a study may not necessarily (and it would be advisable not to expect it to) provide *direct things for copying;* but it can certainly provide nourishing food for thought, which might lead to the right application of the lessons learnt to achieve desired results. An examination of the systems touched upon in Chapter X tends to show that in some of the new territories the most desirable or satisfactory solution may lie only in the proper selection, marriage and adaptation of practices found in more than one other country.

The right choice of pattern cannot, however, be an end in itself.   By far the most decisive thing for success in local government is good administration, which in turn is dependent upon a lot of factors among which may be mentioned the quality of the staff, of the councillors, and the degree of popularity and confidence that a particular local government body enjoys in its locality.   With the first two factors named we have dealt adequately in this book. We have also dealt with the question of popularity, and the main purpose of devoting a whole chapter, as well as of making a few other references to, the old system of Indirect Rule was in order to show, *among other things*, certain features in it which increased its unpopularity. This, of course, was not all we did, for we tried also to point out, though with understandable inadequacy, the successes and failures of the system which might provide useful lessons.

Returning to the question of efficient administration, it might be added that, to help our new councillors, some form of organized training might be arranged for them with considerable advantage. The need for this has already been widely felt in many parts. Such courses of training would, of course, be of very short duration. The scope of such training should not be anything near the scale of what already exists for the senior established staff of the local government bodies. It might prove ideal to conduct such courses on either a divisional or a provincial basis, possibly after every local government election. The subjects to be covered would, naturally, depend on local needs; but they might include such things as relationship of council and staff, finance, council procedure, and so on.

There was one question we purposely failed to answer when we discussed 'mobility' of local government staff, and that was who should see about the effecting of such transfers. Transfers are, of course, of two kinds. There is one in which a staff officer, of his own accord, applies for a transfer to another council possibly to fill a higher post. If he is accepted by this new council, it should not be difficult for the two councils concerned to arrange between themselves for such a transfer to take place under suitable conditions. There is the other kind of transfer—let us call it a routine one. Such transfers used to take place under the old Native Administration system and the person responsible for effecting them used to be the Administrative Officer in charge of the Division or Province concerned. Depending on whatever local arrangement may exist, such transfers might be effected when and where necessary by the Resident (in Eastern Nigeria), Local Government Inspector (in Western Nigeria), Regional Officer (in the Gold Coast), etc., in charge of the area concerned. Where these offices no longer exist (for who can tell the future?) or where the officers concerned are not given the necessary authority to do this, the Ministry concerned might be responsible for doing it.

Further to our general advice against the introduction of party politics into local government, particularly in less advanced areas, Nigeria's recent experience clearly showed that if local government administration is tied to national political parties any unhappy relationship between the parties on a national basis is bound to have unpleasant repercussions on local government administration. The ghost of the political crisis of 1953 in Nigeria loomed disastrously over the heads of the big local government bodies, even after the national crisis had been virtually resolved. The number of difficulties that can result in such a state of affairs can best be appreciated by imagining a situation where the national government is controlled by one party and a local government body by another. It might be difficult in such a situation to expect very cordial relationship to exist between, say, the Minister of Local Government and a local government body controlled by the Opposition Party.

Finally, political parties are always in open competition with one another. They are rival bodies, always in a sort of race and afraid to be outdone by their opponents. In the heat of a political race there is always the tendency and risk of forgetting or losing sight of local practicabilities and realities. This may lead to the making of unreasonable promises, as when would-be rural district councillors promise their electors that, once elected to office, they would provide their constituency with all the social amenities available in big municipalities, but without the people having to pay more

167

tax, or even as much as they are at present paying! Such promises are quite impossible to fulfil, but they are quite possible to make when different political party candidates try to make themselves more acceptable than their opponents whom they must discredit. The subsequent frustration that must be the lot of their electors, from their obvious failure to redeem the fantastic promises, cannot, to say the very least, be a good omen for the success of local government. Politics can be fostered and encouraged in the great councils of State, where it may well be a democratic *sine qua non*, but they might well be excluded from local government councils where the field for political races is all too limited or even non-existent. What is needed in the new councils is not a political race, but a sure and steady movement up the ladder of progress and development.

Good luck to Local Government in Africa!

APPENDICES

NOTES ON THE FUTURE OF THE ADMINISTRATIVE SERVICE

WITH the rapid progress of many colonial territories towards independence, many people, both in Britain and in the Colonies concerned, are worried about the future of this versatile and hard-worked service. But nobody appears to have a cut and dried answer to any question that may be put about the future of the members of that Service who seem to have been hard at 'working themselves out of their jobs'. All seems so uncertain.

Through the mist of uncertainty, however, two schools of thought are discernible—one negative and the other positive. The one regards administrative officers as a sort of scaffolding which is used when building is in progress, but which must be removed once the building has been completed. Administrative officers were used, the argument goes on, to build up the territories to political independence and once this is achieved they should no longer be necessary and so must be removed. None of the supporters of this school of thought seem to be able to say precisely when the 'scaffolding' should actually be removed—before, on, or immediately after the attainment of full self-government by the territories? All of them seem agreed, however, that wrong timing may be disastrous.

The other school of thought holds that, even with the attainment of self-government, the offices of administrative officers should be retained, for they have become an accustomed and trusted political institution of the territories concerned. But here too, no one has been able to say exactly what should be the new position and status, as well as functions, of the officers. Vaguely they feel their position and functions would be 'more or less' the same—which is not helpful enough.

No matter from what angle one looks at it, the position is hardly satisfactory or fair. It is particularly unfair to the younger serving officers whose career is directly affected. A definite assurance one way or another would be preferable, and is very desirable, since it would enable a young man in the service to know early whether to consider a change in career or not.

All, of course, will depend on the attitude of the territories themselves when they become self-governing. The attitude of the Colonial Office to the territories attaining independence in respect of officers appointed by the Secretary of State, might be put in the following way: 'It all depends on you. If you feel that these men will be useful to you, and you really need them, I am prepared to allow those who are willing to stay on to do so, subject, of course, to reasonable safeguards about their rights and benefits, for I cannot disown my responsibility for them. If you don't want them, they will not stay. But, remember that it will mean the ruin of a life's career in many cases, for which they are, in equity, entitled to reasonable financial compensation.'

The final word must rest with the individual colonies concerned. Judging, however, from recent examples it is not difficult to see which way the wind blows in the colonial territories affected. The Sudan and the Gold Coast have proudly retained that branch of the Civil Service. In Nigeria the unfriendly words and attitude of some years back are now generally replaced by kinder and appreciative ones from national politicians—there is no indication that anyone seriously wants administrative officers to go. If one can draw an inference, it is that everybody now seems fully to realize the very important (almost indispensable) position that these officers occupy in the administrative machinery of the countries concerned. Rather than diminishing, the importance of these officers has grown as the various countries approach full nationhood. Even professed critics of 'yester-year' are now under no illusion that they can lightly dispense with the services of these officers without undesirable consequences. What evidence is there in support of these inferences? How do we know that administrative officers previously generally looked upon as 'agents of imperialism' are now generally popular?

One glaring piece of evidence only will answer these questions. Whenever a dependent country is about to become independent the branch of the service most urgently desired to be 'nationalized' is the Administrative Service. This urgent insistence on 'nationalization' cannot be anything but evidence of the supreme importance attached to the Service. Like the secret (or other security) service it is considered too delicate and important to entrust indefinitely into the hands of 'expatriates' who sooner or later will have to leave.

The Gold Coast, unlike the Sudan, is not carrying out her own scheme of 'nationalization' of the Service by indiscriminate replacement of 'expatriates' with 'non-expatriates'. What she has done, since a few years ago, is to ensure that there should be no further pensionable recruitment of expatriate officers to fill vacancies which might occur. There can be no doubt that this is a more judicious move than that taken by the Sudan in asking all their expatriate officers to go, and replacing them by Sudanese with small regard to qualifications and experience.

Administrative work is in itself a highly specialized occupation. Those who sometimes speak of administrators as not being as useful as *technicians*, do not seem to appreciate the special nature of administrative work. No country can be successfully governed by *technicians*. Good administration is governed not by formulas but by a quick ability to assess and judge values. It requires great mental skill and is far more delicate at times than any ordinary technical duty, because it directly affects human beings and their

problems. It also requires special education and temperament as well as the possession of the right sense of human
touch. It is a vocation. Much more than in ordinary
technical professions mere possession of academic or professional qualifications is not enough to ensure success—this
must be supplemented with other qualities, which makes it
necessary that prospective entrants into the service should
be very skilfully selected.

The writer has once heard a leading personality arguing
that boys from secondary schools were 'qualified enough' to
do the work of a District Officer! Anybody who knows
that the standard qualification for admission into that
branch of Civil Service has in the past been, at least, a
good university degree, and also knows that this educational
requirement was not in any way superfluous, will realize at
once how ignorant the maker of the statement was of the
work and responsibility of administrative officers.

It should be seen from what has been said in the last
two paragraphs why we have said that the approach of
the Gold Coast to the problem of the highly desirable
'nationalization' of Administrative Service was more
judicious than that of the Sudan. (See, however, the next
paragraph.)

'Nationalization' should not be allowed to lead to a
serious fall in standards, which can only be ensured through
proper caution. Since in none of the nations now emerging
to a state of independence can there be enough men with
the necessary qualifications and qualities to fill all the
vacancies that would occur in the event of wholesale departure of the present expatriate holders, it would be most
highly desirable that, pending the building up of their own
stock of administrators, the new nations now being born
should be neither afraid nor ashamed to make use of the
experienced services of those serving 'expatriate' officers
*who are willing and happy to stay on and serve them as loyally and
faithfully as they were doing before the changeover. Given goodwill
and understanding on both sides there is no reason why such people*

should not be available, even with the generous retiring arrangements available for them. It is such men whom the new and inexperienced indigenous candidates can usefully understudy—and such understudying is indispensable for future successful administration. *Far from being a sign of continued dependence upon external power, the staying on of such officers would be good evidence of goodwill existing on both sides.*

The attitude of the Sudan and of the Gold Coast have been mentioned above. There is an important difference to note existing between the Sudan and other colonial territories such as the Gold Coast and Nigeria. And it is this: The Sudan has obtained her independence *outside* the Commonwealth, while the Gold Coast, Nigeria, etc., want their independence *within* the Commonwealth. If members of this great family of nations have the mutual understanding which should exist within one family, it follows that no person from any section of the family should regard himself or be regarded as a foreigner (if that can be substituted for the already overworked word 'expatriate') in another section. All of them would strive to help one another in any way possible. And that is why we count ourselves among those who feel, as well as hope, that the more senior members of the family will not deny the younger members all necessary assistance and co-operation, in any field necessary, even after the latter have come of age and taken their full places as adult members of the family.

The future of the Administrative Service then is a *positive* one. It can now be reasonably assumed that in scarcely any of the present colonial territories will Administrative Service *as such* be unwanted, after independence. It has been seen that the tendency everywhere is to 'nationalize' rather than to abolish the Service. Another tendency is perhaps the hardly very relevant one of changing the titles of the members of the Service. In the Gold Coast the District Commissioner of old is now formally known as Government Agent, while the Resident is known as Regional Officer. In the Western Region of Nigeria, these two officers are respectively styled Assistant Local Government Inspector and Local Government Inspector. The main reason for these changes appears to lie in an attempt to give the impression that their position has changed—that they are no longer 'agents of imperialism', but servants of the people. Commenting on this tendency, Mr. R. E. Wraith in his *Local Government* (p. 109) has these noteworthy remarks to make:

> The thing that is worth remembering behind all these surface changes is that the greatest virtue of the office of D.C. or D.O. was its *flexibility*—its ability to adapt itself to changing circumstances. The new titles are rather more formal than the old: it is to be hoped this does not mean that the flexibility will depart, and that the new man, be he European or African, will become a bureaucrat treading a well-worn path. In the fluid circumstances of West Africa there is a great need for versatile men, of independent judgement and character, who can be called upon to interpret to the ordinary people the changes which are bound to follow one another in quick succession . . . .

It does not appear that it matters materially what titles the officers of the Service bear (although there would hardly be any harm in leaving them alone). What matters is what their actual functions and position should be. The main virtue of Administrative Service, as the above passage shows, has in the past lain in its *flexibility, adaptability and versatility*. As long as it is clearly realized that their usefulness would be curtailed if their position becomes too formal or specialized they might be given any title on earth.

In the main body of this book the position and functions of administrative officers *vis-à-vis* local government bodies have been discussed. An attempt was made to show that the new relationship should be governed by the motto 'Leadership, education and guidance from within' and not 'Control and direction from without'—a situation, it was felt, which should be governed by what Mr. Wraith would describe as 'personal relationship rather than constitutional rights', except perhaps where delegated functions are dis-

176

charged. It was also suggested that delegation of some powers vested in the Governor or the Minister might with advantage be made to Administrative Officers who are nearer the spot, and so on. It is not necessary to elaborate on these suggestions again, except perhaps to allay one rather common fear, which is that the bringing in of administrative officers into the new local government systems would drive out ordinary men of ability and education who would otherwise have been quite willing and happy to serve on the councils. It is difficult to see why this should happen if the administrative officers played the role which has been suggested in this book. That, however, is in connection with local government about which the responsibility of administrative officers must remain more or less secondary. What about their position and proper functions as central government officials?

It has been said that if the usefulness of this Service is to be retained, its flexibility, adaptability and versatility should not be seriously, if at all, interfered with. It follows that the position of the officers as general representatives of the Central Government might be continued very much in the present form, but with one important difference. *Instead of being looked upon as the 'rulers' of the people, they should ostensibly be what might be described as the executive arm of the Government or Cabinet.* In this capacity they would act in and for their Division or Province, as the mouths and ears of the Government—the *intelligence* officers of the Government. They should fulfil the 'great need for versatile men, of independent judgment and character, who must be called upon to interpret to the ordinary people the changes which are bound to follow one another in quick succession'. In turn, they should also interpret the ordinary people to the Government, keeping the latter regularly and fully informed of the reactions and feelings of the former, particularly in regard to Government's intentions and measures. Any Government which must succeed, or which wants to discharge its responsibilities and duties properly and well, should be able to have readily at its disposal such unbiased and properly assessed reports and information, quite apart from having its policy and programmes properly interpreted to the people, particularly in countries where the majority of the people are illiterate and so are untouched by newspapers and the radio.

Internal security, as at present, might remain the first and foremost concern of administrative officers. There would be the miscellaneous duties such as community development, native courts (where applicable), and so on. His powers and functions as Magistrate or J.P. might, of course, continue.

If Administrative Officers generally represent the Government, it would follow that in their Division or Province they must take close interest in what is happening in other departments. And this brings to mind the statement of Lord Milverton (then Sir Arthur Richards), Governor of Nigeria, to the Legislative Council meeting in Lagos in March 1945. Part of the statement read as follows:

> It seems to me that the administration is too loosely knit and that a lack of general co-ordination had deprived Government efforts of some of the effective force which comes from joint effort. . . . The present Government intends . . . to insist that at each level of the Administration the administrative officer-in-charge, whether it be . . . the Resident or the Divisional Officer, *must be regarded as the Captain of a team which works together for the benefit of the people and the progress of the country, and as such he must be in a position to co-ordinate effort without, of course, in any way interfering with the technical achievements of an accepted purpose.* . . .

True, the political conditions of Nigeria have changed many times since the above statement was made. But after omitting (as has been done) those sections of the statement which can hardly be acceptable to modern Ministerial forms of Government, what remains is not entirely without relevance to our discussion. The portion italicized is particularly worth thinking over.

Finally, one is very strongly tempted to see in our future

178

Administrative Service, if properly harnessed, a vitally possible source from which to draw and train members of the future diplomatic service. This is no wishful thinking —it is what is strongly possible. It would all depend on how the service as a whole is built up and harnessed. With the majority of the members as natives, closely connected with the Government of the day, capable of understanding and interpreting Government policy efficiently, and knowing the people and their psychology intimately, there could be no better source of diplomatic choice than this.

We now go back to the point raised earlier in these notes, namely the qualifications that those entering the service should have. There can be no doubt that for a person to be able to discharge the functions and responsibilities such as have been sketched, special qualifications must be necessary—educational and otherwise. If facts must be boldly faced, one should not be afraid to say that nobody would be qualified for appointment to the service who had not had a university education plus good character and ability OR had had long and tried experience in the junior stratum of the Service and was of proved ability and character. To relax these requirements would be to compromise efficiency and good administration.

With planning and looking ahead, there is no reason why suitable arrangement could not be made with the University Colleges, which now exist in nearly every territory, so that special training for prospective candidates should not be overlooked.

But, and this is a big BUT, it must not be forgotten that to attract the right type of men into the particular Service under discussion, there will have to be *real* inducements— inducements and attractions which salaries alone, no matter how generous, cannot provide.

SECTION 99 OF THE LOCAL GOVERNMENT ORDINANCE OF EASTERN REGION OF NIGERIA (1950)

THE Regional Authority may by Instrument declare that, subject to such limitations and conditions as he may impose, a council either shall perform or may perform all or any of the following functions in respect of the area for which it is established:

Agriculture

(1) Provide services for the improvement of agriculture.
(2) Control methods of husbandry.

Animals

(3) Prohibit, restrict or regulate the movement in or through the area of the council of any livestock.
(4) Establish, maintain and control pounds, seize and impound any stray animal, and provide for the payment of compensation for damage done by such animal.
(5) Prohibit cruelty to animals, and any specified acts of cruelty to animals.
(6) Prohibit, restrict and regulate the keeping of livestock of any description.
(7) Prevent and control the outbreak or the prevalence of any disease among animals.
(8) Provide services for the improvement of livestock.

Buildings

(9) Prescribe the conditions subject to which the erection and construction, demolition, re-erection and construction,

conversion and re-conversion, alteration, repair, sanitation and ventilation of public and private buildings and structures may be undertaken and carried out.

(10) Provide for building lines and the layout of buildings.

(11) Make advances upon such conditions as shall be thought fit for the purpose of enabling rate-payers to build or to buy dwelling houses.

(12) Prepare and undertake and otherwise control schemes for improved housing layout and settlement.

(13) Prescribe the conditions to be satisfied by a site for any building or for any class of building.

(14) Prohibit the construction of any new building unless and until the plans thereof have been submitted to and approved by, the council.

(15) Provide for the demolition of dangerous buildings if necessary at the expense of the owner, or occupier, and provide for the recovery of such expenses.

(16) Prohibit or regulate the use in any defined area of any inflammable material in the construction or repair of any building.

(17) Build, equip and maintain social centres, public libraries, communal feeding centres, restaurants, catering and other rest houses, or buildings designed and used for public purposes.

(18) Build, equip, maintain and let shops.

(19) Prohibit or regulate the making of borrow pits or other excavations.

(20) Control and regulate the siting of advertisements and hoardings or other structures designed for the display of advertisements.

Education

(21) Build, equip or maintain any Primary school.

(22) Grant sums of money towards the establishment, equipment or maintenance of any Primary school.

(23) Grant and maintain scholarships or bursaries to

suitable persons to attend any school or other educational institution in Nigeria or elsewhere.

(24) Provide for the compulsory education of children or of specified categories of children between the ages of five and fourteen years.

(25) Grant sums of money towards the establishment or maintenance of any public library, museum or to any association existing for the promotion of arts, and crafts, or recreation and sport.

Forestry

(26) Establish and maintain tree nurseries, forest plantations and forest reserves and sell the produce thereof.

Land

(27) Prevent and control soil erosion.

(28) Provide for the fencing of land and for the maintenance and repair of such fences.

(29) Require any person to cultivate land to such extent and with such crops, as will secure an adequate supply of food for the support of such person and of those dependent upon him.

Liquor

(30) Prohibit, restrict, regulate or license the manufacture, distillation, sale, transport, distribution, supply, possession, and consumption of palm wine and any kind or description of fermented liquor usually made by the natives of Nigeria or in the adjacent territories.

Markets

(31) Build, equip, open, close and maintain markets and prohibit the erection of stalls in places other than markets.

(32) Regulate and control markets including the fixing of and collection of stallages, rents and tolls.

(33) Fix the days and hours during each day on which a

market may be held and prevent the sale and purchase of goods in markets on any day or at any hours except those fixed.

Public Health

(34) Safeguard and promote public health including the prevention of and the dealing with any outbreak or the prevalence of any disease.

(35) Build, equip, and maintain, or grant sums of money towards the establishment, equipment or maintenance of any hospital, maternity home, dispensary, asylum for the aged, destitute or infirm or for orphans or asylums and settlements for lepers.

(36) Exterminate and prevent the spread of tsetse fly, mosquitoes, rats, bugs and other vermin.

(37) Establish and operate ambulance services.

(38) Establish, install, build, maintain, and control drains, latrines, public lavatories and wash places and any sewage systems.

(39) Establish, maintain, and carry out sanitary services for the removal and destruction of and otherwise dealing with nightsoil and all kind of refuse.

(40) Provide, erect and maintain a public water supply, regulate or prohibit the sinking of wells and provide for the closing of wells.

(41) Prevent the pollution of the water in any river, stream, water-course, water hole or drain and prevent the obstruction of any river, stream or water-course.

(42) Build, manage, license and control slaughter houses.

(43) Regulate the slaughter of and provide for the inspection of animals intended for the food of man.

(44) Regulate the preparation and sale of meat.

(45) Establish, maintain and control cemeteries and burial grounds.

Public Order

(46) Prohibit any act or conduct which in the opinion of

the council is likely to cause a riot or any disturbance or a breach of the peace.

(47) Prohibit, regulate or restrict the carrying and possession of weapons.

(48) Prohibit, restrict and regulate the migration of persons from or to the area of the council.

(49) Prevent fires and control grass-fires.

(50) Establish and maintain fire brigades and provide for the use and custody of any appliance for the extinguishing of fires.

(51) Prohibit or regulate gambling.

(52) License and regulate guides, porters and carriers.

(53) Control the movement of beggars in streets and public places.

(54) Suppress brothels, disorderly houses, and take measures to prevent prostitution.

(55) Prohibit, restrict or control the hawking of wares.

(56) Regulate and control public collections in streets and public places.

Registration of Persons

(57) Provide for the registration of persons residing within the area of the authority of the council or in any part thereof.

(58) Require the marriage, birth or death of any person within the area of the authority of the council to be reported to or registered with the council and to appoint registration offices and registrars for such purposes.

Roads, Streets, etc.

(59) Make, alter, divert and maintain roads, streets, paths, culverts, bridges, street-drains and water courses.

(60) Provide or arrange for lighting in public places.

(61) Regulate all traffic in the area.

(62) License bicycles and vehicles other than motor vehicles including motor bicycles.

(63) Establish, provide and maintain parks for motor and other vehicles.

(64) Require persons to carry lights during certain hours in certain areas.

(65) Establish, acquire and maintain transport services by land or water including ferries.

(66) Regulate or prohibit the planting, cutting, tapping or destruction of any trees or vegetation growing along any street, road or path or in any public place.

(67) Provide that the owner or occupier of any land or tenements maintain clear and keep free from vegetation the roads, streets or paths adjoining their land or tenements.

(68) Regulate the naming of roads and streets and the numbering of houses.

Trade and Industry

(69) Prescribe the conditions under which any offensive trade or industry may be carried on.

(70) Prescribe the conditions of employment in factories, workshops, bakehouses, eating houses and laundries.

(71) Fix the maximum price which may be demanded in the sale by retail for any article of food in any market.

(72) Establish, erect, maintain and control public weighing machines and other instruments of measurement.

Various Matters

(73) Protect, preserve and prohibit the removal from any place of any African antique work of art.

(74) Regulate child betrothals.

(75) Establish, control and manage recreation grounds, open spaces and parks.

(76) Provide for the maintenance of any traditional office or customary title which is on the date of the commencement of this Ordinance receiving such maintenance, or which is recognized by a vote of three-quarters of the total membership of the council in the area.

(77) Provide for the licensing of any suitable building or other place for the performance of stage plays, cinematograph films or other public entertainment and to prescribe

the conditions under which such plays, films or entertainments may be shown.

(78) Prescribe the duties of any person employed by the council in connection with any function of such council.

(79) Prohibit, restrict or regulate the capture, killing or sale of fish or any specified kind of fish.

(80) Erect, extend or alter any pier subject to the provisions of the Piers Ordinance (Cap. 170).

(81) Grant sums of money to Associations existing for the benefit and welfare of children and young persons.

(82) Perform any function for the provision of the peace, good order and welfare of the persons within the area of the authority of the council, which may, by notice published in the Gazette, be sanctioned by the Governor, whether such function is similar to those enumerated in this section or not.

NOTES ON THE NEW LOCAL GOVERNMENT ORDINANCE OF EASTERN REGION OF NIGERIA (No. 26 OF 1955)

SINCE the draft of this book was completed and sub-mitted to the publishers, the Eastern Regional Govern-ment of Nigeria has passed a new Local Government Ordinance which replaces the old one of 1950. The reason for this, according to official explanation, is that 'experience of local government has shown that the (old) law is deficient in some respects and it has been found necessary to make many changes in the Local Government Ordinance of 1950'. Since, therefore, it was not possible to take them into account while discussing the various points raised in the book, it would be useful here to summarize certain aspects of this new Ordinance, which are relevant to our discussion in the main book, for the benefit of readers.

(i) *Control*

The new Ordinance, which is divided into eighteen Parts, with appendices, transfers all the powers and duties originally vested in the 'Regional Authority' (i.e. the Governor) to the Minister, who in some instances will exercise these powers with the approval of the Governor-in-Council, in other words, with the approval of the Executive Council. Under the new law the control of the Local Government bodies by the Central Government through the Minister has been greatly tightened. For instance, whereas under the old Ordinance a Council had unlimited powers to enter into contracts, under the new law a Council may not enter into contracts, which by their terms will involve a Council in an expenditure of more than *one hundred pounds*, without the approval of the Minister, or somebody acting on his behalf.

Of far reaching importance in the new Ordinance is the power of the Minister to dissolve a Council and order a fresh election. Under the old Ordinance, if a Council were too bad to be allowed to go on, the Regional Authority could only revoke the Instrument establishing such a council; now the Minister can either do this or dissolve the council as already stated.[1]

Local Government Commissioners. A very important feature of the new Ordinance is the provision for the appointment of what are known as *Local Government Commissioners* to whom, with a few reservations, the Minister can delegate such of his functions as he may think fit. An official explanation to this move says, 'The experience of three years has shown that not a few councils are very immature and inexperienced, while some are incompetent and worse. The control exercised from the Ministry is too remote to be effective and there is at present no machinery by which the Minister can easily and readily obtain information about what is going on in the councils. The appointment of Local Government Commissioners will provide the necessary link and will enable a stricter and closer control of councils to be exercised by the Minister.' (Compare our views on the question.)

(ii) *Types of Councils*

There shall be five types of Councils—County Councils, Municipalities, Urban District Councils, District Councils, and Local Councils.

(iii) *Establishment*

All these Councils shall be established by Instrument

---

[1] The procedure, under the old Ordinance, was for the Regional Authority to issue an Amending Instrument which would both dissolve the Council and either establish a new council under the provisions of the Ordinance or appoint suitable persons to serve as a 'Caretaker' Council.

issued by the Minister with the prior approval of the Governor-in-Council. The Instrument apart from specifying the name, type, seal, area and constitution of each council, may specify how a particular council can run or administer its business as well as lay down what functions the councils *shall* or *may* perform.

(iv) Functions

Apart from certain functions (such as the maintenance of law and order) which councils are obliged to perform, the functions laid down in Section 80 of the Ordinance are permissive rather than mandatory. The Minister is given the discretion of deciding what functions any particular Council *shall* or *may* perform. In other words, *all* councils will not be required to perform the same functions or duties but will rather be assigned such duties as the Minister may consider appropriate for the particular area concerned. This part of the Ordinance contains all the functions contained in Section 99 of the old Ordinance—*vide* Appendix B —with some additions.

(v) Composition

Unless otherwise specified in the Instrument, Councillors are to be elected, but an Instrument may provide for some or even all of the Councillors to be appointed rather than elected. This provision for *appointment* is of far-reaching importance and may be a means of satisfying the need, which we have strongly advocated, of getting men and women whose knowledge, experience or social position can be of advantage to the councils, on to the Council. (Compare our views on the subject.) The Ordinance makes it obligatory for Municipalities to appoint Mayors and Deputy Mayors.

Term of Office of Councillors. The Ordinance provides that the term of office for councillors shall be three years. No provision is made, as in the old Ordinance, for one-third of the Councillors to retire each year, to ensure continuity of administration. But under a saving clause the Instruments establishing Councils under the 1950 Ordinance are still effective unless cancelled or revoked by the Minister. This means that the provision for one-third retirement each year may remain for some time yet.

(vi) Committees

County Councils, Municipalities, and District Councils *are required* to appoint Finance Committees and (unless otherwise provided in the Instrument) Medical and Health Committees. In the case of the latter the Minister is empowered to specify the composition of such committees including the number and qualifications of any members who are not members of the Council. A Council may in addition to these statutory committees appoint other committees. A committee may include members who are not members of the council provided that two-thirds of the members of every committee shall be members of the council. In addition a committee may *co-opt* persons who are not members of the council to be members of such committee, but such co-opted members will be entitled to no votes. A Council may concur with one or more councils in appointing from among their respective members, members of a joint committee of such councils for any purpose in which they are jointly interested.

Delegation of Powers to Committees. A council may delegate to any committee with or without restrictions or conditions any functions that can be exercised by the council, except the powers of making bye-laws, levying a rate, issuing a precept or borrowing money.

Under Section 5 (2) (j) the Minister can insist, under certain circumstances, that persons who are not members of the councils *shall* be appointed to committees of a council.

(vii) Staff

The Law requires every County Council and every Municipality (subject to the approval of the Minister and the provisions of the relevant part of the Ordinance) to appoint a Medical Officer of Health for the area of its authority. (For District and Local Councils, which may not be able to afford the services of a Medical Officer of Health, the Ordinance empowers the Minister to appoint, after consultation with the Minister of Health, any fit persons, to serve the areas as Medical Officers of Health. This provision would enable Government Medical Officers to be appointed to serve the areas affected.) It also makes it the duty of a council to engage and pay adequate staff for any Native Court for the maintenance of which such council is made responsible under the provisions of the Instrument under which it is established. As regards other categories of staff the Ordinance empowers a council, subject to the approval of the Minister, to appoint such officers, engage such staff and employ such persons as it shall consider necessary for the efficient discharge of its functions. After appointment no person employed by the council can be dismissed for any reason without the approval of the Minister in writing.

As regards conditions of service for the Local Government Staff the Ordinance empowers the Minister to draw up 'Staff Regulations' which may provide for:

(a) maintaining discipline;
(b) regulating appointments, remuneration, increments, promotion, termination of appointments, dismissals and leave;
(c) regulating the payment of allowances, the grant of advances, and the terms and conditions of service generally;
(d) providing for the transfer of staff or any employee from the service of one council to that of another and regulating the conditions of such transfer;
(e) such other matters relating to departmental procedure and the duties and responsibilities of officers as the Minister considers can be best regulated by such regulations.

Any such regulations in so far as they relate to discipline may in particular provide for:

(a) withholding or deferring of increments, or reductions in rank or salary either permanently or for a stated period;

(b) the deduction from salary due or about to become due of such sum as may be appraised in respect of damage to property of a council by misconduct or breach of duty on the part of an officer.

Local Government Service Board. Of still greater importance is the provision for the appointment of Local Government Service Board to whom the Minister or any council may (either generally or specifically) refer for advice in matters relating to appointment, discipline, etc., of staff. Subject to the provisions of the Law the Minister may make regulations providing for:

(a) the appointment, tenure of office and terms of service of members of the Local Government Service Board;

(b) the organization of the work of the Board and the manner in which it shall perform its functions;

(c) consultation by the Board with persons other than the members of the Board; and

(d) the appointment, tenure of office, and terms of service of staff to assist the Board in the performance of its functions.

The Board shall consist of a Chairman and four members to be appointed by the Minister. (We have quoted this particular portion of the Ordinance *in extenso* because it seems to support our own arguments in the book—*vide* p. 136.) The Ordinance also makes provisions for other matters affecting staff, such as age of retirement, provident fund, gratuities, etc.

(viii) *Finance*

The main sources of revenue for councils, of course,

remain the same under the new Law as under the old.
They include:

(a) all sums of money or funds as are granted to a council
by the Minister under the provisions of Sections 221
and 230;

(b) revenue accruing to a council from the following
sources:

(i) moneys derived from licences, permits, dues,
charges or fees, specified by any bye-law made by
a council;

(ii) moneys payable to a council under the provisions
of any other written law;

(iii) receipts derived from any public utility concern,
service, or any undertaking belonging to or maintained by a council either in whole or in part;

(iv) rents derived from the letting or leasing of any
building or land belonging to a council;

(v) grants-in-aid out of the general revenue of the
Eastern Region, or other public revenue;

(vi) any particular public revenue which may lawfully be assigned to a council;

(vii) any sums of money which may lawfully be assigned
to a council by any public corporation;

(viii) interest on the invested funds of a council;

(ix) receipts from the sale of lands; and

(x) fees, fines and penalties payable in respect of or
as a result of proceedings in any Native Court
which a council is required to maintain and the
proceeds of sale of any forfeitures ordered by such
Native Court.

Municipalities and District Councils remain the rating
authorities, while County Councils and Local Councils can
only precept on District Councils. There are two important provisions in the new Ordinance concerning precepts
by County Councils. The first is that a District Council is

now empowered to appeal to the Minister against a precept imposed by a County Council, and the Minister has the power to vary such precept if he is satisfied that the appeal is justified. The second provision is that if a County Council issues a precept to more than one District Council, the amount required from each District Council shall be related to the number of persons living in the area of such Council.

The estimates of expenditure are rigidly controlled by the Minister who, in addition to his powers to vary, amend or reject such estimates, may now give *conditional* approval to Local Government estimates of expenditure.

A class of officials known as *Examiners of Accounts* may be appointed by the Minister. The officials are to have access to a Council's records and accounts at any time within office hours for the purpose of 'advising the Minister or any such council either generally or specifically'.

(ix) *Relationship between County and District Councils*

A County Council may, with the concurrence of the District Council within the area of its authority, delegate to such District Council, with or without restrictions or conditions, any of its functions under the law *except*:

(a) functions for the discharge of which the County Council is required to appoint a committee; and
(b) the power of borrowing money or issuing a precept.

In discharging such delegated functions the District Council shall act as Agents of the County Council.

If it appears to a County Council that a District Council within its area has failed in the performance of its functions conferred by the Instrument establishing such District Council, the County Council shall complain to the Minister.

Steps to be taken by the Minister on receiving such complaint are laid down in the Ordinance. (These provisions are not new, being present also in the old Ordinance.)

(x) *Miscellaneous*

As can be easily understood, the above cannot and should not be taken as a full summary of the voluminous document which runs into 230 Sections, with many appendices. The points briefly summarized are those which bear direct reference to what have been discussed in this book—and even so it cannot be claimed that all such points have been touched. For a detailed study (which we would recommend) readers are referred to the main Ordinance, copies of which can easily be purchased from the Government Printer or recognized booksellers which deal in Government publications.

It was not our intention or place to comment on the Ordinance. But let us say that there are some people who feel that the new Ordinance marks a step backward from the old one. We find it difficult to share this view which appears to emanate from the undesirable habit of thinking that what does not follow a well-known pattern practised elsewhere is not good enough. (We have said enough about the undesirability of such an attitude in the book.) For our part we feel that the present Ordinance is, at least, more *realistic* than the former one, taking into account the needs of the Regions.

BIBLIOGRAPHY

The following is a list of books for supplementary reading:

Awolowo, O. *Path to Nigerian Freedom.* Faber, 1946.

Azikiwe, N. *Political Blue Print for Nigeria.* Ziks Press Ltd. Lagos, 1943.

Batten, T. R. *Problems of African Development, Part II.* O.U.P., 1949.

Busia, K. *Position of Chiefs in Ashanti.* O.U.P., 1951.

Cameron, Sir Donald. *Native Administration in Nigeria and Tanganyika.* African Soc. Journal, Vol. 36, November 1937.

Cameron, I. D., and Cooper, B. K. *The West African Councillor.* O.U.P., 1954.

Cary, Joyce. *Britain in West Africa.* Longmans, 1946.

Chapman, B. *Introduction to French Local Government.* Allen & Unwin, 1953.

Cole, G. D. H. *Regional and Local Government.* Cassell, 1947.

Dimock, M. E., & Dimock, E. O. *American Government in Action.* Rinehart & Co., Inc., N.Y.

Drummond, J. M. *The Finance of Local Government.* Allen & Unwin, 1952.

Gardiner, R. K., and Judd, H. O. *Development of Social Administration.* O.U.P., 1954.

Hailey, Lord. *Native Administration in British African Colonies.* H.M.S.O.

Jackson, W. E. *Local Government in England and Wales.* Penguin, 1945.

Jennings, Sir Ivor. *Principles of Local Government Law.* U.L.P., 1947.

Macmillan, W. M. *Africa Emergent.* Penguin, 1949.

Mair, L. P. *Native Policies in Africa.*
Native Administration in Central Nyasaland. (Official Publication.)

Robson, W. A. *The Development of Local Government.* (Third edition.) Allen & Unwin, 1954.

Wraith, R. E. *Local Government.* Penguin, 1953.

British Commonwealth Objectives. Imperial Institute of Royal Society of Arts.

INDEX

Accounts, Examiners of, 194
Administrative appeal, 101
Administrative Officers (District Officers), 140–4; future of, xii, 74, 171–9; native Africans barred as, 28–9; relation of, to Native Authorities, 41–2, 141, 143; duties of, 59, 86, 109, 118; delegation of power to, 141, 177; relation of, to Councils, 141–4, 176–7; qualifications of, 141, 174, 179; as executive arm of Government, 177–8
Administrative Service, future of, 171–9
Advisory Councils to Emirs of Northern Nigeria, 32; of indigenous chiefs, 35–7
Afforestation, 76, 91, 182
Africa, political development in, 14, 18–19, 31; early local government systems in, 18; European scramble for, 26; racial discrimination in, 29–30; poverty of, 77, 79, 81
Africans, effect of war-time experiences on, 19; question of welfare of, 27–8; discrimination between Europeans and, 28–30; educated, and indigenous organizations 37–8
Age-grades, 37, 120, 123
Agriculture, loans for, 78; local government functions regarding, 180
Akidas of Tanganyika, 34
Aldermen, 117
Amanyanibo of Opobo, 120, 123
Animals, local government functions regarding, 72–3, 180
Arochuku, Eze of, 120, 123
Atlantic Charter, 19–20
Audit, power of, 101–2

Azikiwe, Dr. Namdi, *Political Blueprint of Nigeria* of, 28–9

Berlin Conference (1885), 26
Bourdillon, Sir Bernard, 22
Bribery in elections, 113
British local government, copied in Africa, 15–16, 68, 164–5; organization of, 53–5, 60, 61–2n; redistribution of functions in, 64–5; State grants for, 67n, 84–5; functions of, 78; Coles on, 74–5; Robson on, 75n; State control of, 101–2, 161–2; Committee system of, 115, 140; Aldermen of, 117; party politics in, 127; appointment and control of staff in, 132, 134; relation between Council and staff in, 139; voluntary service in, 146–7; history of, 160–2
Buildings, local government functions regarding, 180–1

Calabar, Obong of, 36, 119–20, 123; hydro-electric power in, 52; Co-ordinating Agencies for, 62
Cameron, Sir Donald, 27, 32, 33, 39, 109
Central Government, and expenditure, 42, 98; source of power of local council, 48, 50, 80; essential services and, 52, 66–7, 79; delegated functions of, 74, 77, 141–2, 177, 188; and local government services, 80–1; and finances under Indirect Rule, 83; Grants of, 84–5, 87, 98; taxes payable to, 85–7, 98; contribution of, in lieu of rates, 89–90; and loans to local authorities, 90, 98; functions of

District Officer (*see* Administrative Officers)
Divisional Councils, 123

Education, local government and, 66, 72, 76, 78–9, 181–2; free primary, 70, 79; compulsory, 80, 182
Election of Councillors, 53, 110–115; corrupt practices in, 112–15
Electricity, provision of, 52
Entertainment allowance, 147
Enugu, 59
Equalization Grants, 85
Examiners of Accounts, 194
Eze of Arochuku, 120, 123

Fees, 92, 193; increased, 96–7
Finance, local government, 82–94; poverty of, 82; under Indirect Rule, 82–3; Committees, 140, 190; provisions under 1955 Ordinance, 192–4
Fines and penalties, 92, 193
Forest Reserves, 76
French local government, 150–5; history of, 162
Fulani conquest of N. Nigeria, 32

German rule in Tanganyika, 34
Gold Coast, local government reforms in, ix, 164; British connection with, 30; chiefdoms of, 32n; decentralization in, 106; election to local government bodies of, 111; traditional authorities on councils of, 119, 123; retains Administrative Service, 172–6; change of titles in, 175–6
Goldie, Sir George, 27–8
Governor (*see* Regional Authority)
Grants, Central Government, 84–85, 87, 193; Code, 86; Ministerial power to withhold, 101
Great Britain, post-war attitude of, to colonies, 13–14, 19–20; chartered companies of, 26–7; humanitarian and religious influence, 27; political training in local government bodies of, 51; loans to Local Authorities in, 90; derating in, 98–9; party

Great Britain—*continued*
politics in local councils in, 127.
See also British local government.

Health: Services, 66, 76, 79; Committees, 190
Hospitals, 78–9

Ibadan, 59
Ibibio, Nkukus of, 36; Mbong Ikpa Isong or Clan Heads of, 36, 40–1, 120, 123; age-grades among, 37; Native Administration among, 39
Ibibio State Union, 40
Ibos, Obis and Igwes of, 36; age-grades among, 37; Native Administration of, 39
Igwes of Ibos, 36
Income tax, 85, 87–8; local, 97–9, 101
Indirect Rule, 16–18, 164; divergent views on, 25–6, 42–3, 108; origins of, 26–8; Administrative Service under, 28–30; nationalist distrust of, 30; benefits conferred by, 31; ignores indigenous authorities, 33–8; position of Native Authorities under, 41–2, 109–10; avoids raising oligarchy of ruling classes, 44; epitaph of, 44–5; finance under, 82–3; conservatism of, 108; French system compound with, 150–2
Investment of surplus funds, 93–4
Irish local government, 137, 148–150, 157, 162–3

Jennings, Sir Ivor, 48–9
Joint Committees, 129; on appointments, 135–6; on conditions of service of staff, 136
Judicial control, 102; French, 154

Kaduna, 59
Kenya, 29–30, 164
Kwa Falls, 52

Lagos, 33, 59; taxation in, 85–6; Town Council of, dissolved, 104; Mayor of, 123–4

INDEX

Native Administration, 15, 18. *See also* Indirect Rule

Native Authorities and central legislature, 22–4; create new chiefs, 23; need for central control over, 24; and Clan Heads, 40–1; 'Advisory Bodies' to District Officers, 41–2; Annual Estimates of, 42; expenditure of funds of, 93; membership of, 108–9; exclusion of members from local councils, 117; relation of District Officer to, 141, 143

Native Courts, 76, 92, 191–3

Ndichies, 37, 120

Niger Company, 27

Nigeria, position of indigenous chiefs in, 22, 36–7, 43–4; Richards Constitution in, 22–3; high costs of local government in, 58–9; County Boroughs in, 59–60; poverty of local government finance in, 82; taxes in, 85–6; overseas investments of, 93–4; party politics in, 124–5, 167; future of Administrative Service in, 172–3

Nigeria, Eastern Region, democratic local government started in, ix, 68–9; Indirect Rule in, 31, 33–40; 'warrant chiefs' of, 34–6, 38–9; Women's Riots in, 35–6; 'constitutional' heads of, 36–7, 39, 43–4; local government reforms in, 39–40, 163–4; electricity for, 52; taxation in, 86, 88–9; surplus funds of, 93; control of local authorities in, 102–6; elections in, 111, 117; traditional authorities in, and local government, 119–20; appointment and control of local government staff in, 132–3; voluntary service in, 144–5

Nigeria, Eastern Region, Local Government Ordinance of (1950), 69–72, 180–6; (1955), 106n, 111n, 112n, 187–95

Nigeria, Northern Region, Indirect Rule and Emirs of, 32–3; District Officers in, 42

Nigeria, Western Region, local government reforms in, ix, 164; chiefdoms of, 32n; District Officers in, 42; decentralization in, 106; traditional authorities on councils of, 119, 123; change of Administrative titles in, 175–6

Nkas, 37

Nkukus of Ibibios, 36, 40

Ntoes of the Quas, 36

Obi of Onitsha, 120–1

Obis of Ibos, 36

Obong of Calabar, 36, 120–1, 123

Oji River, 52

Onitsha Province, hydro-electric power in, 52; Co-ordinating Agencies for, 62; Obi of, 119–120, 123

Opobo, Amanyanibo of, 120, 123

Otu-okpokolos, 37, 122

Party politics in local government, 124–8, 167

Percentage Grants, 85

Phillipson, Sir Sidney, 82–3

Port Harcourt, 60

Precepts, by Village (Local) Council, 88, 193; by County Councils, 193–4

President of local council, 120n., 147

Property, rates on, 95–6

Provincialization, 138–9

Public Health, 183

Public Order, 183–4

Quas, Ntoes of the, 36

Rates, 88–90; difficulties regarding, 77–9, 81; Government Contribution in lieu of, 89–90; unfairness of, 95–6; site, 97; levying of, 193

Regional Authority (Governor), Eastern Nigerian, powers of, 102–6; and Native Authorities, 109; duties transferred to Minister, 187–8

Regional Local Government Association, 136
Regional Officer, 167, 175
Regional Planning Authorities, 74–5
Registration of persons, 184
Resident, and Village Councils, 72; and taxation, 86; and election of Councillors, 111, 112n; and dismissal of Councillors, 152; and transfer of staff, 167; Captain of a team, 178
Richards Constitution, 22
Roads, 76, 184–5; village, 72
Robson, W.A., regional councils of, 75n
Rural District Councils, British, 53–4; Nigerian, 58, 60, 62; power of Regional Authority over, 104
Rural Districts, rating difficulties in, 89, 95; election of Councillors in, 111

Sanitation, public, 66, 183
Schedule: One Tax, 85; Two Tax, 85–6
Scholarships, 78
Site rates, 97
Social services, local government and, 14–15, 24, 51–2
Staff, Local Government, 131–4; Regional Authority's power of sanction of appointment of, 104, 132; appointment and control of, 132–3, 135–6; payment of, 134–5; conditions of service of, 136, 191; security of, 137; mobility of, 138, 166–7, 191; relations between Council and, 139; under 1955 Ordinance, 190–2; disciplining of, 192
Standing Administrative Committee, Swedish, 155
Sudan, Administrative Service in, 172–5
Suffrage, women's, 87; universal adult, 111
Surcharging, 146
Swedish local government, 155, 162

Tanganyika, 33–4
Taxation, direct, 85–8
Town Clerk, 112, 133, 139
Towns, rise of cosmopolitan, 20; local government in, 50, 59–61; and rural areas, 60; likelihood of new, 61; election of Councillors in, 111–12
Trade and industry, local government's functions regarding, 185
Trading loans, 78
Transfer of staff, 138–9, 166–7, 191
Transfer value, 138
Travel allowances, 146

Uganda, 164
Umudiabas, 37
United States of America, local government in, 156–9, 162
University Colleges, 179
Urban Councils, Gold Coast, 111
Urban County Council, Onitsha, 119–20
Urban District Councils, British, 53–4; Nigerian, 58, 60, 62, 188; power of Regional Authority over, 104
Urban Districts, rating in, 89; election of Councillors in, 111–12

Village Councils, 55–6, 62; functions and powers of, 70–3, 79; 'precepts', 88; revenue earning assets of, 91; election to, 111, 121; position of traditional authorities regarding, 120–3; compared to American counties, 158
Village heads and local councils, 120–3
Voluntary Agencies, 72, 79
Voluntary service, 144–7

Wandirobo tribe, 33
Warrant chiefs, 34–6, 38
Water supply, 76; and local government, 52, 183
Women, taxation of, 87–8; eligible as Councillors, 110
Women's Riots (1929), 35–6, 38
Wraith, R.E., *Local Government* of, x; 176

For Product Safety Concerns and Information please contact our EU
representative GPSR@taylorandfrancis.com
Taylor & Francis Verlag GmbH, Kaufingerstraße 24, 80331 München, Germany